Adventure Cycling™ in

Michigan

Selected On- and Off-Road Rides

Adventure Cycling™ in

Michigan

Selected On- and Off-Road Rides

The Adventure Cycling Association

THE
MOUNTAINEERS

Published by
The Mountaineers
1001 SW Klickitat Way, Suite 201
Seattle, WA 98134

The Adventure Cycling Association
150 E. Pine Street
Missoula, MT 59807-8303

1 0 9 8 7
5 4 3 2 1

Published simultaneously in Great Britain by Cordee, 3a DeMontfort Street, Leicester, England, LE1 7HD

Manufactured in the United States of America

Edited by Julie Hall
Maps by The Adventure Cycling Association
Cover design by Amy Peppler Adams, designLab—Seattle
Book design by Alice Merrill
Book Layout by Virginia Hand
Cover photograph: © Gregg Adams Photography
Frontispiece: One of the many rail-trails in Michigan (photo by: Laurie James)

Library of Congress Cataloging-in-Publication Data
Adventure cycling in Michigan : selected on- and off-road rides.
        p.   cm.
    Includes index.
    ISBN 0-89886-505-0
    1. All terrain cycling–Michigan–Guidebooks. 2. Cycling–Michigan–Guidebooks. 3. Michigan–Guidebooks. I. Adventure Cycling Association.
GV1045.5.M5A33   1997
796.6'3'09774—dc21   97-8534
                                                          CIP

Printed in Canada

Contents

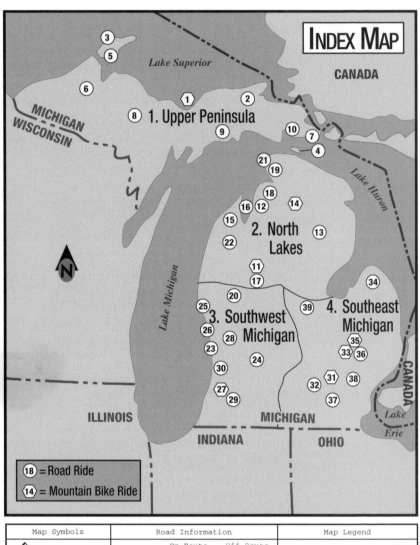

INDEX MAP

Lake Superior

CANADA

MICHIGAN
WISCONSIN

③
⑤
⑥
⑧ 1. Upper Peninsula
① ②
⑨
⑩ ⑦
④

Lake Huron

㉑
⑲
⑱
⑯ ⑫ ⑭
⑮
㉒
2. North Lakes
⑬

Lake Michigan

⑪
⑰
⑳
㉞
㉕
㉖
㉓
㉘
㉙
㉗
㉚
3. Southwest Michigan
㉔
㊴
4. Southeast Michigan
㉟
㉝ ㊱
㉜ ㉛ ㊳
㉟
㉜ ㊲
㊳
CANADA

N

ILLINOIS
MICHIGAN
INDIANA
OHIO

Lake Erie

⑱ = Road Ride
⑭ = Mountain Bike Ride

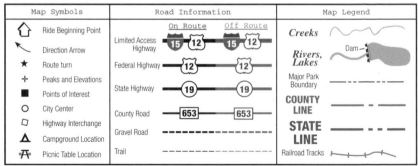

Map Symbols		Road Information		Map Legend	
⌂	Ride Beginning Point		On Route Off Route	Creeks	
↖	Direction Arrow	Limited Access Highway	🛡15 🛡12 🛡15 🛡12	Rivers, Lakes	Dam
★	Route turn	Federal Highway	🛡12 🛡12		
✚	Peaks and Elevations			Major Park Boundary	
■	Points of Interest	State Highway	⑲ ⑲	COUNTY LINE	
○	City Center	County Road	653 653		
⬜	Highway Interchange	Gravel Road		STATE LINE	
△	Campground Location				
⛩	Picnic Table Location	Trail		Railroad Tracks	

Preface

The rides in this book were submitted by members of the Adventure Cycling Association, a national association of more than 40,000 individuals who love using their bicycles for exploration, discovery, and adventure. Based in Missoula, Montana, Adventure Cycling has for more than twenty years mapped the back roads of the United States expressly for cyclists and has created and helped maintain a national network of bicycling "highways."

Many cyclists do not have the weeks or months required to undertake the long-distance, coast-to-coast routes that Adventure Cycling has

Riding along Lake Cadillac (photo by: Bruce Baker)

created. There is a need for many shorter, quality rides that cyclists can complete in a day, a weekend, or a short vacation. One of the aims of this book is to provide cyclists with information about such rides.

Bicycling continues to be one of the fastest growing activities in the country. The well-known rides—especially those near urban areas—are attracting more and more cyclists every year. Yet thousands of miles of good riding, both on and off pavement, go virtually unused. Another aim of this book is to identify excellent but little-known cycling opportunities. In directing cycling enthusiasts to new routes, we hope to reduce cycling traffic on well-known trails.

To compose this guide, we asked our members to nominate their favorite rides in Michigan. Each contributing member has ridden the trail he or she described and collected the route information along with accommodation listings, ideas about what to see and do, and special notes about the ride. You can meet the contributing cyclists in the About the Contributors section at the back of the book.

Maps for the book were prepared by the Adventure Cycling staff based on information supplied by contributors. Keep in mind that recent road or trail construction—or natural phenomena—may have changed the trails somewhat since the descriptions were written. For this reason, when appropriate, we have listed other maps and information sources to supplement the maps in the book.

We have worked hard to provide a wide variety of tours, including rides suitable for cyclists of all skill levels. Rides range from a few hours to several days, and the descriptions specify whether they are appropriate for road bikes or mountain bikes.

Acknowledgments

We want to thank the members of Adventure Cycling who submitted their favorite rides for our consideration. There were many fine rides offered that would not fit into this volume.

Several people on the Adventure Cycling staff were involved with the production of this book:

- Tom Robertson, our cartography department assistant, did the lion's share of collecting the routes from members, reviewing rides, and assembling the final selection with input from other staff members. Tom also completed a lot of the work on the maps.

- Carla Majernik, director of the cartography department, developed the mapping approach and designed the initial templates that were used in the production of the maps. The final product—clean, readable, and useful—is what we have come to expect from Carla in her twenty-plus years of developing maps for Adventure Cycling.

- Gary MacFadden, executive director of Adventure Cycling, compiled the narrative using descriptions supplied by the members and wrote the introductory sections of the book. Gary loves both on-pavement and off-pavement riding and was itching to get some use out of his journalism degree.

- Jennifer Hamelman, our assistant cartographer, did quite a bit of work in drawing, sizing, and proofing the maps. Jennifer is an avid tandem bicycle enthusiast, as well as a top-notch computer guru for Adventure Cycling's routes and mapping department.

We also want to acknowledge the efforts of Julie Hall, who copyedited the manuscript, and the staff at Mountaineers Books, who designed and produced this handsome volume.

Introduction

Michigan is a state whose destiny has been shaped by water. Retreating glaciers sculpted the landscape and carved out the river channels. The surrounding Great Lakes and river ways led early explorers and missionaries to Michigan's shores. Later the rivers became water highways for the lumbering industry, and the lakes became connections to other ports for importing and exporting goods. The surrounding waters even determine Michigan's temperate climate, which has been so important to the development of its fruit orchards.

The state name reflects the area's abundance of water: *Michigan* is taken from *michi gami*, an Algonquin phrase meaning "large lake." Four of the Great Lakes lap at the state's shores: Lakes Michigan, Huron, and the western end of Lake Erie enclose the Lower Peninsula; Lakes Michigan, Huron, and Superior define the Upper Peninsula.

Together these lakes form approximately three-fourths of the state's boundary and provide Michigan with approximately 2,400 miles of shoreline on navigable waters—more than any of the other contiguous forty-eight states. Michigan also claims 833 miles of island shoreline.

Michigan's numerous rivers are relatively short. In the Lower Peninsula, they flow smoothly over well-worn beds; in contrast, the Upper Peninsula's rivers are turbulent and rushing as they strive to reach the Great Lakes. The most impressive falls are those of the Tahquamenon River; the swift St. Mary's River also has a series of spectacular falls and rapids.

The largest of the approximately 11,000 lakes in the state lie within the Lower Peninsula; these include Burt, Charlevoix, Houghton, Mullett, and Torch Lakes. The major rivers are also in this portion of the state: The Grand, Kalamazoo, Manistee, Muskegon, and St. Joseph Rivers all flow into Lake Michigan. Except in a small area in the western part of the Upper Peninsula, all Michigan streams flow into the Great Lakes, and then into the Atlantic Ocean through the St. Lawrence Seaway.

EARLY EXPLORATION

For hundreds of years before the arrival of Europeans, Native Americans of the Algonquin tribes inhabited *michi gami*. They hunted red fox, black bear, rabbits, beaver, and white-tailed deer and traded the skins with neighboring tribes. The trade in animal skins eventually contributed to the downfall of the Algonquin's peaceful lifestyle. Word of the valuable resources to be found in the region reached Samuel Champlain, the Lieutenant Governor of New France. In addition to furs, Champlain was interested in finding copper, as well as a shortcut to the Far East.

Champlain sent Etienne Brulé to explore the area in the early 1600s. After this initial exploration, more explorers and missionaries made their way to Michigan, one group after furs, the other after the souls that they perceived needed saving.

One early missionary, Father Jacques Marquette, established Michigan's first permanent white settlement at Sault Ste. Marie in 1668 and a second mission at the Straits of Mackinac in 1671. Marquette later explored much of the Mississippi River Valley, opening additional areas for settlement.

No serious effort was made at European settlement in the area until 1696, when Antoine de La Mothe Cadillac convinced King Louis XIV of France that the Lower Peninsula could support permanent communities and was awarded enough soldiers, men, and supplies to start a colony.

Fort Mackinac (photo by: Jim DuFresne)

The Grand River channel (photo by: Arthur "Doc" Souter)

In 1701, La Ville d'Etroit, "the village of the strait," was founded. It quickly became an important trading post, attracting trappers, traders, businesspeople, farmers, and speculators. Detroit, Michigan's first city, had been established.

Control over the Michigan region was variously claimed by French, British, and American colonists, as well as, of course, by the original Native American inhabitants. In 1783, the Treaty of Paris awarded the area to the newly independent United States. Settlement continued and was given a huge boost by the opening of the Erie Canal in 1825. The population more than tripled in the decade between 1820 and 1830.

STATEHOOD

If the Upper Peninsula had not been used as a bargaining chip to bring Michigan into the Union, today the Upper Peninsula would most likely be part of Wisconsin. In 1834, with trade flourishing and communities growing, the territorial legislature applied to Congress for statehood. The petition was blocked because Ohio, which had become a state in 1803, also laid claim to a narrow strip—470 square miles—of land southwest of Detroit that contained the town of Toledo. The border dispute raged in the halls of Congress for months. Ohio representatives were joined by representatives of several southern states who feared that Michigan would enter the Union as a "free" state, upsetting the precarious balance of slave and free states. Finally, a compromise was struck: Michigan and Arkansas would enter the Union simultaneously, the former as a free state and the latter as a slave state. Ohio was to be given the "Toledo Strip," and Michigan would be given the Upper Peninsula, which at the time was a section of the Wisconsin Territory. While there were plenty of people upset by the compromise, it was later decided that Michigan had made a pretty good "trade." Michigan was officially admitted as a state on January 26, 1837.

ECONOMY
Michigan is one of the foremost industrial and agricultural states. Since its earliest settlement, its economy has been based upon a wide range of products, including fruit, timber, minerals (copper and iron), and automobiles.

Lumbering gained a foothold in Michigan's Lower Peninsula in the early 1800s. Fire had recently swept through much of Detroit, and lumber was needed to rebuild the rowdy metropolis. Crude sawmills that had answered the modest needs of the settlers were pressed into service in the haste to supply lumber for rebuilding Detroit. Michigan's first industrial boom was under way.

In 1834, the first steam sawmill was erected on the Saginaw River; a little more than twenty years later, over five hundred sawmills were in operation in Michigan's vast pine forests or at the mouths of the great rivers that drained them. The cutting reached its peak during the 1880s. Early settlers and lumbermen predicted that Michigan's pine forests could never be exhausted; in fact, they were nearly leveled in only two generations.

The exploitation of Michigan's forests was in some ways similar to what happened during California's gold rush era. Large, boisterous towns sprang up overnight and were gone just as suddenly once the axes fell silent. It is estimated that the lumber barons took in dollars nearly three times what the miners took in gold from the rivers and mine shafts of California.

As the state was still recovering from the demise of the timber industry, a new boom came about. The first decade of the 1900s brought the arrival of the automobile and along with it the creation of the Ford Motor Company, General Motors, and dozens of other smaller manufacturers, many of them centered in the Dearborn and Detroit area. With the introduction of the Model T and Henry Ford's moving assembly line, the automobile was on a roll in Michigan. It is no surprise that America's first paved concrete roads were laid in Detroit.

Manufacturing has dominated Michigan's economy ever since, particularly in the Lower Peninsula. Trucks and trailers, sporting equipment, steel springs, hardware, refrigerators, paper products, and rubber goods all contribute to an economy that had to recover at the turn of the century from the disappearance of lumber resources.

Children examine just-harvested grapes at one of the many wineries on Mission Peninsula. (photo by: Jim DuFresne)

Agricultural products also play an important role in the state's economy. Nearly 80 percent of the nation's red tart cherries are grown in Michigan, mostly in the Grand Traverse Bay region. You may associate cranberry bogs with New Jersey or Maine, but Michigan ranks first in the production of cranberries. Navy beans, cucumbers, potted geraniums, Easter lilies, and blueberries are other important cash crops.

Mining has also been important in Michigan's economic history; the earliest explorers of Michigan found Native Americans mining copper in open pits. Michigan also ranks second to Minnesota in the production of iron ore, taken primarily from the Marquette iron range in the western half of the Upper Peninsula.

GEOGRAPHY

Michigan is the second largest state east of the Mississippi River. Those who do not live there are fond of noting that the Lower Peninsula is shaped like a mitten. Those who do live there are probably tired of having this called to their attention. However, when you have a ready-made map on the palm of your hand, you are bound to use it sooner or later to give a non-Michigander directions to another part of the state.

The Lower Peninsula is 277 miles long and 195 miles wide. Except on the southern end, it is bordered by the Great Lakes and their short connecting rivers. Its topography, in general, is low and gently rolling, with occasional hills and hundreds of lakes and marshy areas. The topography of the Lower Peninsula changes from flat plains in the southeast and the Saginaw lowlands to a moderate plateau in the north. A ridge of glacial deposit—what geologists call a moraine—extends from Mackinaw City to central Michigan, approximately bisecting the northern half of the peninsula. The moraine seldom rises more than 1,500 feet above sea level; its highest point is near Cadillac, where it soars nearly 1,200 feet above Lake Michigan (1,700 feet above sea level).

Glacier-invoked hills are strikingly apparent in Oakland and Washtenaw Counties, where the Huron and Erie glaciers collided and left a jumble of high relief. A similar conflict between the Saginaw and Michigan ice sheets is evident in the counties of Roscommon, Ogemaw, Wexford, and Missaukee. Repeated surges and retreats of ice masses modeled and remodeled the landscape and eventually changed the drainage patterns—waters which had formerly drained toward the Mississippi Valley now flow into the Atlantic Ocean.

Upper Falls at Tahquamenon State Park (photo by: Jim DuFresne)

The Upper Peninsula offers contrasting landscapes. To the south are rolling limestone hills and to the north are sandstone tablelands whose multi-colored sheer walls present some highly picturesque scenery. The western half of the Upper Peninsula is broken, wild, and rugged, while the eastern portion consists of lowlands and swamps. The largest swamp area is that spreading along the Tahquamenon River, which meanders across the central eastern section of the Upper Peninsula.

West of Marquette, the Upper Peninsula rises rapidly to a table-land that, in the green-blanketed Huron Mountains, lies 1,600 to 1,900 feet above sea level. Within this region lie vast iron-ore deposits, and in the northwest corner—the Keweenaw Peninsula—is the strip of copper deposits that enabled Michigan to maintain its lead position among copper-producing states for forty years. Here, along the northwestern shoreline, the Porcupine Mountains rise to over 2,000 feet in elevation.

In this book, Michigan has been divided into four smaller regions: the Upper Peninsula, the North Lakes, Southwest Michigan, and Southeast Michigan. For each of the four regions, you will find a choice of road and mountain bike rides, encompassing a range of riding abilities as well as a variety of cycling experiences. What follows is a quick overview of each region.

Region 1: Upper Peninsula

Compared to the Lower Peninsula, Michigan's Upper Peninsula is rugged, remote, and thinly populated. Many people shorten the term to simply "the U.P." Surrounded by Lakes Superior, Michigan, and Huron, the Upper Peninsula is slightly larger than Massachusetts, Connecticut, Rhode Island, and Delaware combined. The picturesque

Mackinac Bridge (photo by: Jim DuFresne)

shores of the Upper Peninsula are generally rocky, the dunes and beaches being backed by dramatic crags and cliffs.

The region's economy has been shaped—and portions of its landscape somewhat scarred—by various industries, primarily copper and iron mining, logging, and maritime shipping. The Upper Peninsula is best known today for its outdoor recreational opportunities.

It has been proposed several times that the Upper Peninsula become a separate state. Historically, the Upper Peninsula population—many of whom proudly refer to themselves as "Yoopers"—have embraced something of an isolationist attitude. The Mackinac Bridge that connects the two peninsulas is a relatively recent addition. Suggested names for the new state have included "Cloverland," "Hiawathaland," and "Superior."

No matter what it is called, the Upper Peninsula is a delight to visit. When spring arrives—rivers teeming with trout and salmon, forests green and fragrant—vacationers arrive as well. From Memorial Day through Labor Day, much of the Upper Peninsula is filled with visitors; the peak months are July and August. From early September to mid-October there is an autumn color show that rivals anything in New England; this draws a second wave of visitors, though they usually do not fill the parks and lakeside campgrounds as much as in the peak months. Fall also brings hunters, who traipse over the six million acres of land that are open to hunting, in pursuit of deer, black bear, grouse, and bobcats. The long winter months bring cross-country skiers, snowmobilers, and ice fishers to the Upper Peninsula.

Several of the rides in this book center around St. Ignace and Mackinac Island. Mackinac Island lies in the Straits of Mackinac where Lakes Huron and Michigan join. Fearful of an American attack during the Revolutionary War, the British in 1780 moved an entire town from the current location of Mackinaw City over icy waters to the remote island. Here they built a defensive fort that did not become part of United States territory until 1815. Those original townspeople could never have envisioned the annual "invasion" that occurs today as nearly one million visitors flock to Mackinac Island to absorb its rich history and natural beauty. In 1875, Congress created the nation's second national park, comprising about 80 percent of the island's 2,000 acres. This was later transferred to Michigan to become its first state park.

Region 2: North Lakes

Hundreds of miles of shoreline and numerous inland lakes contribute to the North Lakes recreational opportunities. Three counties— Leelanau, Grand Traverse, and Benzie—make up what Michiganders refer to as the Grand Traverse region. It stretches north from Frankfort up the east side of Lake Michigan to the tip of the Leelanau Peninsula, back down to Traverse City, and as far east as a little community with the unlikely name of Acme. (Is this where Wile E. Coyote got all of the materials he used to try to foil the Roadrunner?)

The Old Mission Peninsula juts north from Traverse City, dividing the waters of Grand Traverse Bay into the East and West Bays. This small peninsula was promoted by lumber baron Perry Hannah in the late 1800s and has long been a popular vacation destination for Midwesterners. Old farms and wineries mingle with shops, parks, and beaches. The climate is favorable for farming, and the area boasts abundant orchards and excellent wineries offering free tastings and tours.

Traverse City, at the foot of West Bay, is considered the metropolitan hub of northwestern Michigan and is the area's central destination point; yet it retains an appealing small-town feel, with tree-lined historic neighborhoods and a downtown waterfront. The nationally renowned Interlochen Center for the Arts, just south of Traverse City, hosts a variety of entertainment (see Ride 22).

Just to the north of Grand Traverse Bay and the Old Mission Peninsula is Little Traverse Bay. The towns of Charlevoix, Petoskey, and Harbor Springs dominate the area, which is largely made up of rolling terrain, picturesque farms and orchards, and numerous inland lakes. Since the late 1800s, the Little Traverse Bay region has served as both a lumberman's mecca and a playground for elite families from Chicago, Detroit, and other metropolitan cities. Today the region is one of northern Michigan's finest resort areas.

Region 3: Southwest Michigan

The southwest quadrant of Michigan offers cyclists a wide range of recreational choices. The area experiences cool summers and mild winters. Lots of opportunities in southwestern Michigan revolve around sand and water. Some of the communities, such as Saugatuck, might remind a visitor who has cycled in New England of coastal villages in Maine and Vermont.

Away from the coast, the countryside is a jumble of farms, small manufacturing centers, and rural towns that have yet to recover from the decline of the railroads. The Lower Peninsula has many rail-trails, railways converted to trails for hikers and bikers. Orchards crowd the gently rolling, fertile terrain. Spring is a popular time for cycling here; the colors and fragrances of blossoms are sensory delights. And you can cycle down just about any back road and come across a U-pick farm, cider stand, or winery.

Region 4: Southeast Michigan

First-time visitors to this part of Michigan are surprised to find more than post-industrial forests of blackened smokestacks. Detroit and Flint struggle with the same challenges that afflict many cities in the Rust Belt, but there are still a number of excellent cycling opportunities in southeastern Michigan. One-third of the state's population lives in this region.

Despite its manufacturing reputation, Detroit actually has a very cosmopolitan heritage, befitting its status as the oldest city west of the Appalachians. The flags of three nations—France, Britain, and the United States—have flown over this former trading post. The city served as a chief port of entry for settlers heading for the interior in the mid-1800s and later as a magnet drawing a multitude of immigrants and workers from other parts of America to its booming automobile plants.

A well-designed network of freeways and secondary roads enables the cyclist to get to trailhead destinations quickly. There are plenty of small towns to explore. Port Huron—hometown of inventor Thomas Edison—is just an hour north of Detroit. Here you can watch freighters pass so close you can almost touch them as they travel through a narrow, quarter-mile wide passageway joining Lake Huron and Lake St. Clair. North of Port Huron, situated at the base of the largely rural "thumb" region (remember that mitten shape?), the landscape is honeycombed with farms and small lakeside ports. The region around Saginaw Bay offers wonderful views of Lake Huron and many camping opportunities in county and state parks.

WHERE THIS GUIDE WILL AND WILL NOT TAKE YOU

The rides—especially those in the off-road category—meet two conditions. First, they will not take you across private land. While some

The Pointe Aux Barques Lighthouse at the Lighthouse County Park (photo by: Jim DuFresne)

landowners are willing to let bicyclists cross their land, many are not. Second, they will not take you into wilderness areas. The Wilderness Act of 1964 describes wilderness as closed to "any means of mechanical conveyance." Some bicyclists argue that the bicycle does far less harm to trails than do mules or pack horses, which typically are allowed in wilderness areas. This book is not an appropriate forum for a discussion about the Wilderness Act and its effect on cycling. The recommendations in this book adhere to the current law, good or bad, because there is a lot of great cycling to be had out there without bending or breaking the rules.

DIFFICULTY RATING

No one has yet devised the perfect rating system for bicycle rides. The problem is that no two cyclists are exactly alike. What is difficult for one rider may be another cyclist's typical "tune-up" ride.

To address this ambiguity, we asked each contributor to clearly describe the route, the pavement or trail condition, and the number and severity of climbs. Then we asked them to rate the rides as Easy, Moderate, or Difficult. After reviewing the rides, in most cases we agreed with the opinions of the contributors. In a few cases, we upgraded the level of difficulty.

The rides in the Easy class are short and fairly flat with few (if any) hills. These rides should be fine for novice cyclists or families with younger riders. In the Moderate category, rides will generally include some steep hills or at least rolling hills. Some otherwise flat tours may be rated as Moderate only because they extend over two or more days.

Rides in the Difficult category may involve dismounting to walk up steep grades or to get around large rocks or fallen trees. This last category generally includes the rides with the most climbing.

USING THE MAPS

One or more maps are provided for each ride in this book. The maps are specifically designed to show the featured bike route for each ride and should not be relied on for navigating beyond the route. On each map, a large white arrow indicates the starting point of the ride, and small black arrows indicate the direction of the route as it is described in the corresponding text and ride guide. Note that north is not necessarily pointing up on all of the maps; space limitations and the shape of individual routes necessitated varying the orientation of north. Stars on each map and corresponding ride guide indicate turns in the route. In congested areas, one star on the map may represent several stars (turns) on the ride guide.

COURTESY

In the past half-dozen years, mountain bike sales have exploded. (As of this writing, they account for nine out of every ten bicycles sold to adults.) While most mountain bikers never leave the pavement, the number of people venturing into the backcountry on these capable bicycles is growing, as are conflicts with the more traditional users of hiking trails.

Observe some extra courtesies when bicycling the backcountry. Courtesy comes down to riding with the attitude that you are sharing the road or trail with other users, whether car and truck drivers, hikers, equestrians, or other cyclists. Courtesy also means not harming or disturbing local plant and animal life. The following list of guidelines was developed by the Adventure Cycling Association:

1. Stay on the designated travel corridor and off the vegetation.
2. Yield right-of-way to slower and less mechanized users.
3. Do not cut ruts: Keep off muddy roads and trails.
4. Police your speed and ride in control.
5. Respect trail closures and no-trespassing signs.
6. Leave gates as you found them.
7. Practice minimum-impact travel and camping.
8. Help teach new riders proper trail etiquette.

CLOTHING

Weight and bulk, versatility, and suitability for anticipated conditions are the primary considerations when you are deciding what clothing goes along on your ride. It is important that clothing not restrict your arms and legs, as the constant motion of pedaling can cause terrific irritation.

Shirts and shorts for summer riding give more freedom of movement. When the temperatures drop, switch to long warm-up pants or tights (not jeans) and a windbreaker of breathable, waterproof material. Blue jeans and sweatpants are not appropriate riding attire: Jeans have seams in all the wrong places, and both types of clothing are bulky moisture magnets. Pay special attention to keeping your knee joints warm; they often stiffen easily in chilly weather or during long downhills.

Cycling shorts are possibly the most important investment you can make in cycling attire. Anyone who has experienced discomfort from binding underwear or knotting shorts can attest to the importance of wearing the right thing. What determines whether a pair of shorts is right for you varies considerably according to personal style, body shape, and weight. Check them out around town before heading off for a three-day tour!

On colder days, it is preferable to have several layers of light clothing that can be removed or replaced as the temperatures fluctuate. If you are wearing only one layer of warm clothes, you will be out of luck if the weather suddenly warms, or if you begin to perspire from cycling. A layer of polypropylene next to the body is great for wicking moisture away. (On some people, polypropylene causes an uncomfortable rash. Check it out before you begin an extended ride.)

Cycling shoes are another investment that you might be wise to make if you expect to be doing a lot of cycling. Talk with the people at

Skirting one of the many lakes on Hine's Trail (photo by: Charles Morris)

your bicycle shop about the type of riding you intend to be doing. Some shoes have the pedal attachment built right into the soles; others depend on toe clips and straps to keep the foot correctly situated on the pedal. Many people ride in comfort for years in good-quality athletic shoes and never bother to purchase special cycling shoes. It all depends upon your style of riding.

YOUR BICYCLE

Today bicycles come in a dizzying array of types, each meant for one of two specific types of riding: on-road or off-road. These types are further divided into road racing, hybrid, touring, competition, commuting, club riding, and a few more. You will enjoy the tours included in this book a lot more if you have the right type of bicycle for the type of riding you will be doing.

If you already have a bicycle, match your tours to the bike. If you are shopping for a bike, figure out in advance what type of riding you most want to do. Then get yourself to a bicycle shop (not a general merchandise discount store) and purchase a bicycle that will take you on the types of rides that most interest you.

Wheels and Tires

Another item you will want to carefully consider is tires—where the rubber meets the road (or trail, as the case may be). To escape specific import duties and to give potential buyers a sprightly ride around the parking lot, many manufacturers spec their bicycles with narrow tires. The majority of mountain bikes shipped to bike shops are equipped with 1.5-inch tires. These are too small for tours or even day rides off road, although they will probably hold up nicely for Sunday rides on the local rail-trail. If you are planning to head off road—and you probably are or you would not be reading this book—you will need tires in the 1.9- to 2.5-inch range.

On road bikes, the builders really go narrow on the tires; it seems everyone wants to be Greg LeMond. While narrow tires offer less rolling resistance, they are much more easily damaged, and the time you save by going fast will be lost in patching tires from rim cuts. For off-road riding, you will do much better with 1.25-inch tires, which are available for both the 27-inch and 700C rims. Make sure when swapping wheel and tire combinations that the rubber clears the frame's brake bridges and fenders (if installed), and that the brake blocks still contact the rim and not the tire sidewalls.

SAFETY

Safety should be a primary concern for all bicyclists, especially in the backcountry where it can be difficult to get help in the event of a problem. Keeping informed about current conditions and exercising common sense are the keys to a safe, enjoyable outing.

We recommend that you tell a family member, a friend, or even a park ranger when and where you will be riding and when you expect to return. That way, if you run into trouble, there will be someone to notice your absence and send you help if you need it.

Bicycle Maintenance

Keeping your bicycle in good mechanical condition is key in riding safety. Check it each time you go riding, especially after any disassembly, such as removing a front wheel to install the bike in a car-top carrier. Maybe you put the quick-release skewer back on, but did you remember to reconnect the front brake hanger? Here is a quick mechanical condition checklist:

- Do the brake pads contact the rim properly when closed?
- Are the rims true?
- Are the cables intact, with no fraying?
- Are the tires inflated correctly for the riding conditions you will encounter?
- Are all of the spokes intact?
- Do the wheel hubs turn smoothly?
- Are the handlebars adjusted correctly and locked in position?
- Is the seat adjusted to let you pedal efficiently, with at least 2 inches of seat post still installed in the seat tube?
- Is the seat post locked into position?
- Are the pedals secure on the crank arms?
- Are the toe clips (if you are using them) in good condition?
- Is the chain lubricated?
- Are the front and rear derailleurs working correctly? Are they both tightly attached to the frame?

A quick bicycle check only takes moments before each ride, but it can pay big dividends in safe and enjoyable cycling.

Helmets

The first piece of safety equipment for all bicyclists, whether on or off road, is a good-quality cycling helmet. Wearing a helmet has nothing to do with riding abilities. A skilled cyclist with lightning-fast reflexes can be taken down by a stick, a pavement groove, or even a patch of slippery pine needles. When you start falling is not the time to wish you had a helmet on your head.

A small rearview mirror that attaches to the helmet is also a good investment for riding on a shared-roadway route (shared with automobiles, that is). Any early indication of traffic approaching from behind is a good safety booster.

Sunglasses

Sunglasses or goggles are another good safety accessory. They improve your vision by cutting glare in bright weather, they keep rain and bugs out of your eyes (especially on descents), and they reduce or eliminate tearing in your eyes from wind.

Visibility

When cycling on shared-roadway routes visibility is a prime safety factor. Consider bright-colored clothing, reflective flags, and/or safety triangles (often called "fanny bumpers") as standard equipment—not accessories.

Road and Trail Sense

Practice safe cycling habits, whether on a shared-roadway route or on a backcountry trail. On roads, ride as close to the right as is practical, depending upon the condition of the shoulders or riding lane and obstructions, such as debris or parked cars. You might even pull off the roadway at times to ease the flow of traffic, especially if you get a nervous driver behind you who does not want to pass and causes traffic to back up.

Ride defensively. Pulling off the road or waving cars around you are examples of defensive cycling, an approach to biking that involves anticipating how road conditions and road users will affect your

A familiar view while riding among the Great Lakes (photo by: Gary Wisely)

safety. Planning routes and cycling times is also a part of defensive cycling. Cycling at dusk may be very pleasant, but driver fatigue and dwindling light make this one of the most dangerous times to be on a shared roadway. In contrast, early morning is one of the best times for safe bicycling; traffic often is light, and visibility is better.

Do not just anticipate problems from automobile drivers—hundreds of cycling accidents each year involve cyclists running into other cyclists when riding in a closely spaced pack. On busy roads, keep your bicycles spaced at least two bike lengths apart and ride in a single line. On less busy roads, it is tempting to ride side by side for a pleasant chat with your cycling partner, but you should only do this if the sight distance is long enough and you are visible to approaching drivers from both directions. If the road is curvy and/or hilly, ride single file and schedule more frequent stops for the chatting.

Speaking of stopping, get all the way off the road or trail when taking a break. Road and trail users travel at different speeds. If a cyclist comes hurtling around a corner on a downhill run and you are standing in the trail chatting with a hiker, you are all likely to get injured.

WEATHER

Michigan is fortunate in that its climate is "thermostatically controlled" by the waters that surround it. The Great Lakes—Erie, Huron, Superior, and Michigan—temper the prevailing winds by absorbing heat from air that is warmer than the water and releasing heat when the air temperature drops. Thus, the prevailing westerly winds blow cooler in summer and milder in winter. Few winds can find their way into Michigan without crossing great reaches of water.

The deep waters of Lake Michigan, which rarely freeze over, remain about 39 degrees Fahrenheit regardless of the air's temperature and, consequently, yield heat in winter to the prevailing winds crossing the lake's 80-mile width. This warmth brings heavy snows and makes excessively low temperatures rare. These factors lead to a longer growing season, which has especially benefited the western Lower Peninsula and the cultivation of its orchard belt in the Grand Traverse region.

In nearly all sections of the state, the heaviest rainfall comes between May and October. Thunderstorms are fairly frequent during this season, but tornadoes are extremely rare. Because of the lake-tempered air, the warmest days can dissolve into cool, even bracing, nights, so be prepared with adequate clothing and sleeping bags if you are planning to camp.

The general rule when bicycling is be prepared for just about any weather at any time of the year. If you have chosen your light layers of clothing correctly, you should have few problems. Keep on the lookout for wet weather, especially while cycling at higher elevations. You always face the potential of hypothermia, a condition in which the body's internal temperature has dropped below normal and which can lead to mental and physical collapse. Bicycling in wet conditions is a nearly perfect recipe for brewing hypothermia, which is brought on by exposure to cold and aggravated by wind, wet, and exhaustion.

Hypothermia advances in two stages. The first stage is exposure and exhaustion. The moment your body begins to lose heat more quickly than it can produce it, you are suffering from exposure. Your body begins to make involuntary adjustments to preserve normal temperatures for the internal organs. You also may be inclined to take some voluntary steps to stay warm, such as riding faster or stopping and jumping up and down. This exercise will only prolong and increase your exposure.

Victorian ghosttown (photo by: Jim DuFresne)

At the second stage of hypothermia, your energy reserves are exhausted. The cold reaches your brain stem and eventually the brain itself, depriving you of your ability to reason or make judgments. If the condition remains untreated, you will lose control of your feet and hands, which—if you are still bicycling—will put you in a very dangerous situation. Your body temperature will continue to decrease, eventually leading to collapse and finally death.

The only way to guard against hypothermia is to stay dry. Wool has long been a popular material for bicycling clothes because, even when wet, it retains much of its insulating qualities—much better than do cotton and most synthetics. However, do not trust your clothing to do the entire job. You can get hypothermia even when swaddled from head to foot in wool, if it gets wet enough. Your best front-line protection is a good set of rain gear, including a jacket with a hood, pants, and shoe covers.

BEING PREPARED

Generations of Boy Scouts have survived scrapes in the outback by following the simple rule of "Be Prepared." It works great for cyclists, too. Preparation for the rides in this book falls into three categories: (1) bicycle tools and parts, (2) first-aid supplies, and (3) survival supplies.

Bicycle Tools and Parts

The trick to being prepared is to take what you might really need in order to get out of a jam without taking the whole workbench along. Sooner or later, you are going to need to make an adjustment to a clattering derailleur, replace a bolt, or at least fix a flat tire. Here is a list of basic tools and parts to carry on any outing. They can all fit into a small repair kit that hangs under the saddle or fits in a pocket of a handlebar bag:

- adjustable wrench (6- to 8-inch)
- slotted and Phillips screwdrivers
- nesting tire irons (the three-to-a-set plastic ones work well)
- bicycle tube repair kit
- spoke wrench
- any Allen wrenches suitable for your bicycle
- roll of electrician's tape
- some bike grease (old plastic film canisters work great to hold grease)
- chain tool
- chain lubricant (much lighter than grease)
- small cleaning rag

You should also have the following parts in your repair kit:

- spare tube to fit your tire
- rear brake cable (can be shortened to fit the front brake in an emergency)
- rear derailleur cable (can be shortened to fit the front derailleur in an emergency)
- some extra spokes (three for the freewheel side, three for the opposite side)
- extra chain links (do not bother with these if you decide not to carry the chain tool)
- small freezer bag with an assortment of small nuts, bolts, and washers for racks, brake attachments, water bottle cages, and so on.

First-Aid Supplies

Here is another area of preparation in which you can quickly get carried away. The idea is to have just enough to treat the likely cuts, bumps, and bruises that occur on any outing or even at the backyard barbecue.

Your first-aid kit should include the following:
- sunscreen
- moleskin for blisters
- antibacterial ointment
- 3-inch elastic bandage
- 2-inch roll of gauze
- two triangular bandages
- "second-skin" for burns or road rash
- baking soda for insect bites
- needles and thread
- single-edged razor blade in a blade protector
- insect repellent
- aspirin
- tweezers

Survival Supplies

The survival supplies you will need when biking are the Ten Essentials:
1. waterproof matches or butane lighter
2. compass and map of the area
3. pocketknife
4. extra water
5. extra food
6. rain gear and warm clothing
7. flashlight or headlamp
8. plastic whistle
9. sunglasses
10. "space" (foil) blanket for body-heat retention

To the Ten Essentials, you might want to add water purification tablets. Please note, however, that you should make use of water from mountain lakes or streams only in an emergency. Water from streams and lakes can, unfortunately, make you very sick. An invisible waterborne parasite called *Giardia lamblia* can make you wish you had never gone bicycling. In advanced cases, it can make you wish you had never been born.

You get giardiasis when you ingest a dormant cyst form of this parasite that can live for two to three months in water as cold as 40 degrees Fahrenheit. Many people have the notion that giardiasis is caused by livestock, and that if they are high enough above where cattle might be roaming, the water there is safe to drink. Not true. Giardiasis can be spread by the droppings of horses, squirrels, dogs, cats, beavers, elk, rabbits, deer, and people. In fact, some backcountry studies have suggested that humans may be the most common spreaders of Giardia cysts, simply through improper disposal of human waste.

If you do choose to drink the water from lakes or streams and are smart enough to purify it with water tablets first, do not congratulate yourself too soon on escaping the risk of giardiasis. Purification tablets are not completely reliable, and the cysts can take between three days and four weeks to activate in your intestines. If they do, get ready for severe diarrhea, weight loss, fatigue, the sweats, and cramps. Call a doctor if you spot the symptoms. Drink plenty of fluids but avoid dairy products, which will only worsen your symptoms. There are no well-known home remedies and even the medically prescribed treatments can have unpleasant side effects.

Now, if a refreshing drink from a mountain lake or stream still seems worth all that potential upheaval, all we can do is wish you good luck.

A NOTE ABOUT SAFETY

Safety is an important concern in all outdoor activities. No guidebook can alert you to every hazard or anticipate the limitations of every reader. Therefore, the descriptions of roads, trails, routes, and natural features in this book are not representations that a particular place or excursion will be safe for your party. When you follow any of the routes described in this book, you assume responsibility for your own safety. Under normal conditions, such excursions require the usual attention to traffic, road and trail conditions, weather, terrain, the capabilities of your party, and other factors. Keeping informed on current conditions and exercising common sense are the keys to a safe, enjoyable outing.

The Mountaineers

Region 1:
Upper Peninsula

Cyclists in downtown Cadillac (photo by: Bruce Baker)

Grand Island Shuffle
Submitted by Alan Fark

Grand Island features several criss-crossing trails, including both double- and single-tracks. Most interesting of these is the perimeter trail, which allows you to take in the incredible lakeside vistas while teetering on two wheels on the brink of the sheer sandstone cliffs that encircle the island.

Type of ride: mountain bike
Starting point: Williams Landing on Grand Island
Finishing point: same
Distance: 24.4 miles
Level of difficulty: moderate
General terrain: rolling to hilly
Traffic conditions: no motorized traffic on most of route; however, between October 1 and December 31, ATVs permitted on portions of route, especially during hunting season
Estimated riding time: 3 to 4 hours
Best season/time of day to ride: fall and summer, although mosquitoes and blackflies sometimes extremely bothersome from mid-May to mid-July; Forest Service recommends insect repellent, and head nets for camping
Points of interest: waterfalls, white sand beaches, and Echo Lake, an inland lake teeming with bass, pike, and panfish
Accommodations and services: six designated campsites on Grand Island: two at Murray Bay and four at Trout Bay; dispersed, leave-no-trace camping allowed on much of the rest of the island; no services or potable water on Grand Island; public phone at Williams Landing.
Supplemental maps or other information: available from the Hiawatha National Forest, (906) 387-3700

GETTING THERE
Grand Island is situated in the crystal blue waters of Lake Superior, a half-mile offshore from the Upper Peninsula town of Munising. A private ferry service offers round-trips three times daily in the summer between the mainland and Williams Landing, on the island's south

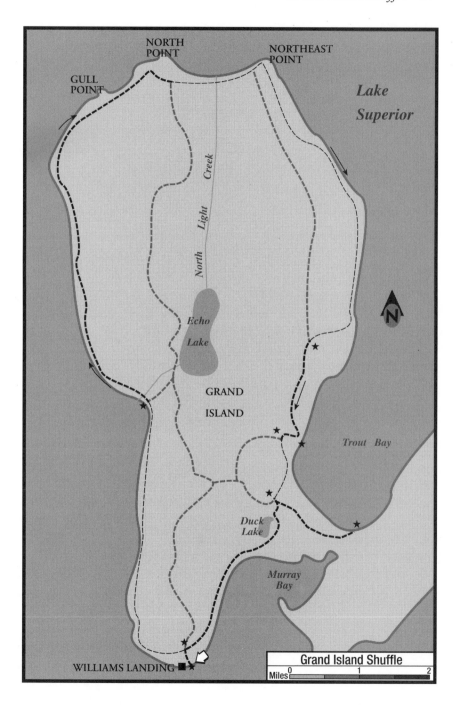

GULL
POINT

NORTH
POINT

NORTHEAST
POINT

Lake

Superior

North Light Creek

N

Echo

Lake

GRAND

ISLAND

Trout Bay

Duck
Lake

Murray
Bay

WILLIAMS LANDING

Grand Island Shuffle

Miles 0   1   2

shore. To get to Williams Landing, take the ferry from Grand Island Landing on the mainland, four miles west of the blinking light in Munising. Munising is located 43 miles east of Marquette on M28. For a current ferry schedule, call (906) 387-2433.

IN THE SADDLE

Until recently, white-tailed deer, bald eagles, and a few lucky cottagers had Grand Island to themselves. Owned since 1901 by the Cleveland Cliffs Iron Company, the island was maintained for decades as a private hunting ground. In 1990, the U.S. Forest Service acquired most of the 13,000-acre island and designated it as a National Recreation Area administered by the Hiawatha National Forest. Today, all but about forty acres of the island are open for recreational activities.

Your ride begins at the point where you disembark the ferry at Williams Landing. Ride north from the ferry landing and immediately turn left onto the bicycle-foot trail. Bear left onto the double-track trail at 4.1 miles. At mile 10.1, bear left again onto the bicycle-foot trail. Bear left at 11.4 miles to continue riding along the trail.

At 16.4 miles, turn left onto the double-track trail. At 17.9 miles, turn right onto the road and then left onto the bicycle-foot trail. At mile 18.7, turn left onto the road and then go straight onto the double-track trail. Turn around at 20.0 miles and, at 21.3 miles, turn left onto the first paved road you encounter. At 22.5 miles, ride onto the double-track trail. Turn left onto the road at mile 24.3, returning to Williams Landing at 24.4 miles.

RIDE GUIDE

- ★   0.0 From Williams Landing, ride north and turn immediately left onto bicycle-foot trail.
- ★   4.1 Bear left onto the double-track trail.
-     10.1 Bear left onto the bicycle-foot trail.
-     11.4 Bear left to continue on the bicycle-foot trail.
- ★   16.4 Turn left onto the double-track trail.
- ★   17.9 Turn right onto the road and then left onto the bicycle-foot trail.
- ★   18.7 Turn left onto the road and then ride straight onto the double-track.
- ★   20.0 Turn around and ride back the way that you came.

★ 21.3 Turn left onto the first paved road.
   22.5 Ride onto the double-track trail.
★ 24.3 Turn left onto the road.
   24.4 Williams Landing. End of ride.

Newberry Ramble
Submitted by Gary Wisely

The area encompassed by this tour is called the great Tahquamenon Swamp and is still one of the wildest sections of Michigan. There are several gravel roads included in this route, so bring your mountain bike or a sturdy touring bike with wider tires.

Type of ride: mountain bike or sturdy touring bike
Starting point: Newberry
Finishing point: same
Distance: 160 miles
Level of difficulty: moderate
General terrain: flat to gently rolling
Traffic conditions: mostly quiet, remote roads with low traffic; about 20 miles of sandy, unimproved roads
Estimated riding time: 4 to 6 days (depending upon if you take an alternate out-and-back side trip to Whitefish Point)
Best season/time of day to ride: mid-June to mid-September
Points of interest: waterfalls, white sand beaches, lighthouse (side trip), Tahquamenon Falls (side trip)
Accommodations and services: Northcountry Campground (4.5 miles north of Newberry on M123, 906-293-8562); Muskallonge Lake State Park (30 miles north of Newberry on M123, 906-658-3338); Tahquamenon Falls State Park (12 miles west of Paradise on M123, 906-492-3415)
Supplemental maps or other information: none

GETTING THERE
Follow I-75 North to the Mackinac Bridge and cross over onto the Upper Peninsula. Eight miles north of St. Ignace, take the M123 exit

and continue northwest for 33 miles. Turn left (west) onto M28 and continue for 24 miles. Turn right (north) onto M123 for 3 miles into Newberry. You can usually park your car behind the offices of the Department of Natural Resources, just off M28 as you turn north toward Newberry (if you want to call ahead, the DNR's number is 906-293-5131).

IN THE SADDLE
Your ride begins in Newberry, a small woodworking and trading center in the Tahquamenon Valley. Lumbering became an economic force in the valley during the Civil War; the Newberry Lumber and Chemical Company was founded in 1882 as a charcoal kiln, which later also distilled wood alcohol and other by-products. Thousands of cords of hardwood were converted into charcoal for use in smelting iron ore. Today, Newberry is a popular base for hunting and fishing expeditions into the forests and cedar swamps of the Upper Peninsula.

If you parked at the Department of Natural Resources (DNR) building south of Newberry and will be spending the first night in Northcountry Campground, pedal to Newberry (1.1 miles) and then on to the campground at Four Mile Corner (another 4 miles). If your first overnight will be at Muskallonge Lake State Park or farther along the route, you should turn left onto H37, an unimproved road at Four Mile Corner.

At Deer Park, turn left again to remain on H37, continuing into Muskallonge Lake State Park. The campground is just about a mile off the main route. As you come out of the state park heading east, bear left at Deer Park to pick up County Road 410 (becomes 414). There are several quick turns along unimproved roads during this portion of the ride, so watch the Ride Guide carefully as you work your way onto County Road 500 (Northwestern Road). At mile 53, turn left (heading east) onto M123.

Just after you rejoin M123, which forms a loop through the Tahquamenon Swamp country, pass the upper entrance to Tahquamenon Falls State Park, located approximately 12 miles west of Paradise. This large state park encompasses 38,496 acres, and includes two falls on the Tahquamenon River. The upper falls are nearly 50 feet

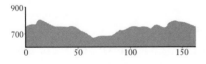

The remains of lumber docks on Lake Superior at the former townsite of Deer Park (photo by: Jim DuFresne)

high and 200 feet wide at the crest; the lower falls, sometimes called the Cataract, are a series of rapids and cascades in three steps with a total drop of 43 feet.

At Paradise, you have the choice to either turn right (south) to remain on M123 or to turn left (north) and spend a day on an out-and-back ride to the Whitefish Point lighthouse, at the head of the bay that shares the same name. It is only an 11-mile ride each way, which should afford you some additional time to ride in and look at the Tahquamenon Falls either before or after riding to the lighthouse.

If you do choose to ride to Whitefish Point, you may wish to visit the ghost town of Sheldrake, just off the route. It is a private town today, so you should check with the proprietors of Curley's Motel in Paradise and tell them you would like to cycle through Sheldrake. They will call ahead and make arrangements. To reach this old logging town that partially burned in 1910, travel 4 miles north of Paradise on M123. Just past the crossing of the Sheldrake River, turn onto the first driveway on your right. You will pass several private houses and then find yourself in Sheldrake. Be careful not to disturb any of the buildings or collect any "souvenirs."

The Whitefish Point post office was established in 1899 for the benefit of fishers operating in Whitefish Bay (obviously named for the type of fish found in its waters). Before the arrival of trappers and commercial fisheries, the Ottawa and Chippewa camped in peace on the shores of the bay, sharing the plentiful supplies of fish there.

Whitefish Point, which extends into Lake Superior, has provided shelter to more than one navigator steering for "the Soo," as the locks at Sault Ste. Marie just to the east are familiarly known. The point breaks the force of heavy seas raised by the long sweep of wind down Lake Superior; in its lee, the waters of the bay remain comparatively calm. The first lighthouse, a brick tower erected in 1849, was replaced at the turn of the century, and a lifeguard station was added. Additional improvements have been made over the years to this key navigational station.

Returning to Paradise, continue south on M123. Approximately 5 miles south of Paradise, the trail crosses the Tahquamenon River, where it empties into Whitefish Bay. This is the former site of the thriving lumber town of Emerson, today the Rivermouth Unit of the Tahquamenon Falls State Park. Millions of board feet of pine were floated down the Tahquamenon River during the lumbering period. The Tahquamenon also figures in literary history: It is believed to be the "dark river" that plays so prominent a role in Longfellow's epic poem *Hiawatha*.

At just over 96 miles into the ride, turn left off M123 onto Curley Lewis Road as you head east onto Naomikong Point. Continuing past Salt Point Road on Lake Shore Road will take you to the Bay View National Forest Campground. Turn around here and head back the direction from which you came, turning left onto Salt Point Road. Salt Point Road will lead you to Strongs and M28, the most highly-trafficked portion of this route. Between Strongs and the Newberry cutoff (M123), M28 winds through young pine forests and cedar swamps and crosses hardwood ridges. Along stretches of the highway, maple and birch line the road on both sides, veiling the scarred lands where the last big trees were logged during the 1930s. The tangled cedar thickets are part of the Tahquamenon Swamp, which reaches north to Lake Superior and Whitefish Bay.

At mile 137, you will reach Eckerman Corner. Eckerman, in its early days, was a supply depot for the district logging camps. Near the end of the last century, there were nearly a dozen camps in the nearby woods, but by 1940 only one sawmill remained. To the north and south of the road is the Hiawatha National Forest.

Midway between Hulbert Corners (mile 144) and McLeods Corner (mile 152.6) is the junction with County Road 381. Leaving the route and turning north here will take you in 4 miles to Soo Junction. Before any highways reached into the virgin timberland to the north, tourists who wanted to view the Tahquamenon River had to abandon their autos at Soo Junction and entrain on a narrow-gauge railway with open cars for the 5-mile trip to the Tahquamenon River. From there, a boat took passengers to the Tahquamenon Falls. The Upper Falls can still be reached by a regularly scheduled combination boat and train ride. The Toonerville Trolley and Riverboat Tour (6.5-hour trip) departs Soo Junction daily at 10:30 A.M., June 15 to October 6.

Continuing west on M28, you will cross lands of the Superior State Forest on your return to the junction with M123 and the end of your ride (assuming you parked at the DNR office).

RIDE GUIDE

★ 0.0 From the DNR office, ride north on M123.
    1.1 Newberry.
★ 5.2 Turn left onto H37.
    19.2 Pine Stump Junction.
★ 27.1 Deer Park. Turn left to continue on H37.
★ 28.2 Muskallonge Lake State Park. Turn around and ride back (east) on H37.
★ 29.3 Deer Park. Bear right to continue on H37.
★ 29.6 Turn left onto Rabbit Patch Road.
★ 31.6 Turn right onto County Road 410.
    34.1 Ride onto Reed & Green Bridge.
    37.1 Ride straight onto County Road 412.
    39.9 Ride straight onto County Road 414.
★ 45.7 Turn right onto County Road 500 (Northwestern Road).
★ 52.9 Turn left onto M123.
    60.9 Tahquamenon Falls State Park.
★ 61.8 Paradise. Turn left onto Whitefish Point Road.

★ 72.9 Whitefish Point Lighthouse. Turn around and ride back the way you came.

　84.0 Paradise. Ride straight onto M123.

　89.1 Emerson.

★ 96.3 Turn left onto Curley Lewis Road.

★ 108.5 Bear left to ride onto Lake Shore Drive.

★ 116.1 Bay View National Forest Campground. Turn around and ride back (west) on Lake Shore Drive.

★ 123.6 Turn left onto Salt Point Road.

★ 134.4 Strongs. Turn right onto M28.

　137.6 Eckerman Corner.

　144.0 Hulbert Corners.

　152.6 McLeods Corner.

★ 159.6 Turn right onto M123.

　160.0 DNR office. End of ride.

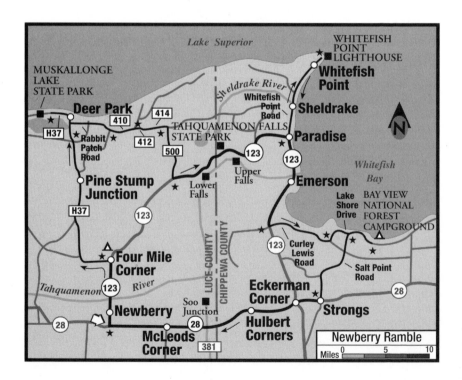

Keweenaw Trek
Submitted by Dan Dalquist

This ride, which begins and ends at the Hancock City Beach, is extremely scenic, particularly in autumn. (For a shorter ride in the same area, see Ride 5, which overlaps the first 16 miles of this 57-mile ride.)

Type of ride: road bike
Starting point: Hancock City Beach parking lot
Finishing point: Copper Harbor
Distance: 57.3 miles
Level of difficulty: moderate
General terrain: rolling to hilly, mostly two-lane road with smooth pavement
Traffic conditions: moderate, except for a 3.9-mile stretch along US 41 with heavier traffic
Estimated riding time: 4 to 5 hours
Best season/time of day to ride: June through September; best to avoid Sundays
Points of interest: scenic views of Lake Superior; Keweenaw National Historic Park, one of the newest national parks in the country; the Sand Hill Signal Station; Brockway Mountain Drive overlook; Fort Wilkins State Park
Accommodations and services: campgrounds, groceries, restaurants, motels, and bike service all available along the route; parking available at the Hancock City Beach
Supplemental maps or other information: available at the Keweenaw Tourism Council office at 326 Shelden Avenue in Houghton; the Keweenaw National Historic Park's guide to a walking tour through the historic business district of Calumet also available at the Tourism office

GETTING THERE
Follow US 41 north through the Upper Peninsula city of Houghton, crossing the Portage Lift Bridge into Hancock. Pass through downtown Hancock to the stop sign near the Citgo service station and continue straight onto M203 for 1.3 miles, to the Hancock City Beach. Park in the parking lot.

IN THE SADDLE

From the parking lot, turn left onto M203, heading north along the Portage Lake Ship Canal. The narrow road winds along the shoreline to McLain State Park at mile 8.6, a good place to stop, top off your water bottle, and enjoy a splendid view of Lake Superior. Turn left when leaving the park to continue north on M203 toward Calumet.

Pass straight through the four-way intersection at 10.2 miles; then begin a 4-mile climb that offers several panoramic vistas of the lake. Especially early in the morning, watch for deer in the fields in this area. At 14.5 miles pass a sign announcing distant Isle Royale National Park, which on a clear day is visible across the lake. Enter the Calumet village limits at 16.2 miles and turn right onto 6th Street to take a short detour through town past the historic Calumet Theatre. Turn left onto Oak Street, passing the Cross Country Sports bike shop; then turn north onto 5th Street. Turn right onto Pine Street (M203) and proceed

The wooden bridge over Eagle River at Sand Dune Drive (photo by: Jim DuFresne)

to the stop sign at US 41. Turn left onto this busy highway and ride north for 3.9 miles, passing the Hut Inn, a good food stop.

At 20 miles, begin the fast and twisting descent into Ahmeek. Where the road levels out, turn left at the Gabriel Chopp Village Park. With the village park on your left, look for the sign to Five Mile Point and turn right onto Bollman Street. Head west past the Cavalry Cemetery at mile 22.6; then cross the Gratiot River. At mile 26.5, the road drops down a ridge to the Lake Superior shoreline. If you are pedaling through in July or August, be sure to stop and pick a snack of wild blueberries, raspberries, and thimbleberries that grow in abundance along the lakeshore.

At 29.4 miles, pass the Sand Hill Light and Fog Signal Station, now a privately owned bed-and-breakfast. Turn left at 33.2 miles onto M26 and enter Eagle River, established as a mining settlement more than 150 years ago. Ride across the new Eagle River bridge; then turn hard right. Take a minute to check out the view of the falls where the river passes under the old highway bridge. The road winds through shoreline forest as it heads toward Copper Harbor, offering tremendous views of the lake and its rocky shoreline and islands. Note how the forest changes with the topography—from cedar swamp, to pine forest, to deciduous stands rich with birch, maple, and aspen. The road has no shoulders and can carry substantial quantities of vacation traffic, but speeds are typically low and drivers courteous.

At Great Sand Bay, 38.1 miles into the ride, the road begins rolling along atop high dunes, proffering big views of the giant lake. Enter Eagle Harbor, where stops of note include the Eagle Harbor Light Station Museum Complex and the Eagle Harbor Store, which opened its doors in 1859. At mile 42.5, a turn into the marina will lead you to North Wind Books, a great spot for browsing and a breather. Deer are commonly spotted in the country traversed over the next 12 miles, so ride sharp in the saddle and you may see some wildlife. At mile 46.0, turn right to tackle the tough 5.1-mile ride up Brockway Mountain Drive, the highest roadway in Michigan—in fact, the highest above-sea-level drive between the Rockies and the Alleghenies. (Those preferring a less strenuous route should continue on M26; see below for description.) On a clear day from the Brockway Mountain summit, 735 feet above lake level, you can see much of the west side of the Keweenaw Peninsula rising out of Lake Superior.

At 51.1 miles, begin the very bumpy and steep descent into Copper Harbor, keeping your speed in check. The overlook at mile 54.8 makes a good place to stop, look down on your destination, and give your wheel rims a chance to cool. At the bottom of the downhill, turn right to enter Copper Harbor, a bustling town brimming with restaurants and shopping opportunities. Attractions and activities include the Fannie Hooe Resort & Campground, lake cruises aboard the Isle Royale Queen, and guided kayak tours. To literally reach "the end of the road," ride 1.5 miles north from the M26 and US 41 junction to Fort Wilkins State Park and then continue for another mile. Outstanding mountain-biking opportunities begin here where the pavement ends, along the dirt road leading to High Rock Bay and Keystone Bay.

Alternate

For those choosing to bypass the grunt up Brockway Mountain, at mile 46.9, pedal into beautiful Esrey Park, where you can scramble over wave-pounded rocks and truly appreciate the raw power of Lake Superior. After one final climb, with the exit from Brockway Mountain on the right and the Copper Harbor Marina on your left, continue to the US 41 intersection (watch for the Thimbleberry Inn). The cumulative distance for those choosing to bypass Brockway Mountain is 55.5 miles.

RIDE GUIDE

★   0.0 From the beach parking lot in Hancock, turn left onto M203.

    8.6 McLain State Park.

   10.2 At four-way stop, continue straight on M203.

★   16.2 Calumet Village. Turn right onto 6th Street.

★   16.4 Turn left onto US 41.

★   21.3 Ahmeek. Turn left onto Hubbell Street and then right onto Bollman Street.

★   21.5 Ride onto Five Mile Road.

   29.4 Sand Hill Light and Fog Signal Station.

★   33.2 Turn left onto M26 into Eagle River.

   42.5 North Wind Books in Eagle Harbor.

★   46.0 Turn right onto Brockway Mountain Drive.

   54.8 Brockway Mountain Drive overlook.

   57.3 Copper Harbor. End of ride.

*Overlooking Lake Superior from the high bluffs of Sand Dune Drive
(photo by: by Jim DuFresne)*

Alternate

46.0 Continue north on M26.

46.9 Esrey Park.

52.4 Hebard Park.

55.3 Ride onto M41.

55.5 Copper Harbor. End of ride.

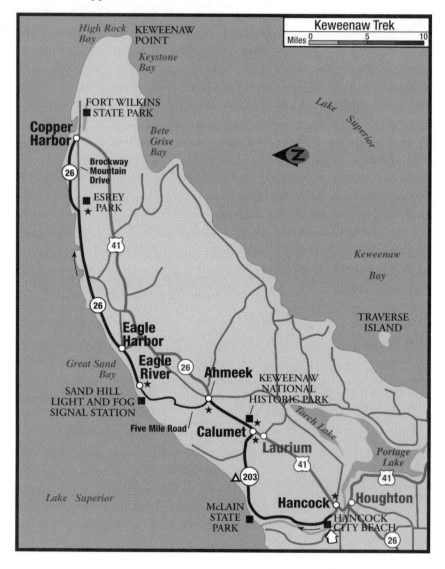

 Mackinac Island Tour
Submitted by John Stevens

This route begins at St. Ignace and traverses the Straits of Mackinac, which connect the Upper and Lower Peninsulas of Michigan, via ferry. Mackinac Island offers a variety of activities and sites, from historic Fort Mackinac to scenic limestone formations.

Type of ride: road bike
Starting point: Mackinac Island ferry dock
Finishing point: same
Distance: 8.4 miles
Level of difficulty: easy
General terrain: follows the island borders with scenic views of Straits of Mackinac and Lake Huron
Traffic conditions: motorized vehicles prohibited on the island, but roads often thick with bicycles and some horses, with and without carriages
Estimated riding time: 1 to 2 hours
Best season/time of day to ride: June through September, any day
Points of interest: limestone formations, Fort Mackinac, Lake Shore Nature Trail, Arch Rock
Accommodations and services: Full services are available at St. Ignace and Mackinac Island. Mackinac Island is a popular destination, so hotel rooms may be scarce: Call ahead for information and reservations. Mackinac has many bicycle shops and bicycle rental places, but do not expect to find quality bikes. Prices for all services are significantly higher than on the mainland.
Supplemental maps or other information: Mackinac Island Chamber of Commerce, Mackinac Island, MI 49757, (906) 847-3783; Mackinac State Historic Parks Visitors Center, Main Street, Box 370 G, Mackinac Island, MI 49757, (906) 847-3328; Michigan Travel Bureau, 333 S. Capitol, Lansing, MI 48933, (800) 543-2937

GETTING THERE
From the Lower Peninsula, follow I-75 to the Mackinac Bridge and cross over to St. Ignace. Take US 2 into St. Ignace, where it becomes State Street, which follows along the waterfront and leads you to the

ferry docks. Parking and valet service are available for your vehicle near the ferries. A round-trip ticket costs about $15, and there are plenty of accommodations for your bicycle on the boat. The trip across the water takes about 15 minutes on a high-speed catamaran, or approximately 30 minutes on a traditional monohull. Ferries depart approximately every 30 minutes during the daylight hours of the spring and summer tourist season.

IN THE SADDLE

Mackinac Island lies between the Straits of Mackinac and the northern end of Lake Huron. The island was originally called *Michilimacinac*, after the French spelling of a Chippewa word meaning "place of the great turtle," which may have referred to the island's outline. Long before the island was settled by the British, the Chippewa supplied the French with furs in exchange for such items as blankets, cooking utensils, and guns.

In 1780, fearful of an American attack during the Revolutionary War, the British moved an entire town from what is now known as Mackinaw City over icy waters to the remote island. The townspeople could never have envisioned that today nearly one million visitors flock to Mackinac Island (pronounced Mac-i-naw) each year to absorb its rich history and natural beauty.

The fort alternated between British and American possession during the eighteenth and nineteenth centuries. The last occupancy by the British was during the War of 1812, when a small party of the King's soldiers arrived unseen at the site of British Landing, hoisted a cannon to the top of the hill, and demanded the fort's surrender, which was granted without a shot.

In 1815, Mackinac Island became a permanent part of U.S. territory, and in 1875 Congress created on the island the nation's second national park. (Yellowstone was dedicated in 1873.) The land, which now comprises more than 80 percent of the island's 2,000 acres, was later transferred to Michigan and became its first state park.

Today, Mackinac Island boasts an active year-round community of about six hundred residents. Once you've landed on the island, step lightly, since the main mode of transportation is the horse-drawn carriage (although bicycles are catching up). Almost all of the food and

Cyclist ready to head uphill past Fort Mackinac (photo by: Jim DuFresne)

supplies needed on the island are brought by ferry from the mainland and then delivered by carriage or bicycle to their destinations.

The island's military history and late nineteenth-century culture come to life inside the walls of Fort Mackinac. This historic fort has been painstakingly restored (fourteen of its buildings are more than two hundred years old). A note of warning: The fort's cannons may be fired numerous times throughout the day as part of dramatic reenactments. While the island's full-time inhabitants have learned to take this in stride, the unexpected blasts can take visitors by surprise.

All ferries arrive in the downtown area of Mackinac Island. You immediately step from the wharves to Huron Street, which during the summer bustles with tourists dipping in and out of the dozen fudge shops found here. Head left or west on Huron Street to skirt the island in a clockwise direction.

Within a few blocks, just after passing Windermere Hotel, Huron Street becomes M185 (or Lake Shore Road, as it appears on many maps). You are immediately rewarded with views of the Mackinac Bridge. At mile 1.5 arrive at Devil's Kitchen, a group of limestone sea caves, and then Lover's Leap, a limestone pillar.

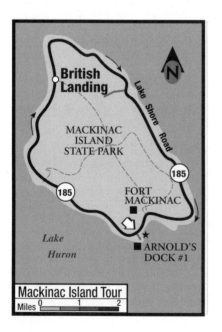

Mackinac Island Tour
Miles 0   1   2

At mile 3.5, you arrive at British Landing. British soldiers landed here on the night of July 6, 1812 in their surprise attack on the Americans. Among the amenities at this intersection are a refreshment stand, the Mackinac Island Nature Center, restrooms, and many benches overlooking the water.

British Landing Road departs M185 here and climbs over the top of the island on its way back to the downtown area. This optional route, on paved road, includes some stiff climbs. There are a number of attractions along the way, including Fort Holmes, the high point of the island where the

British mounted their cannon to take over Fort Mackinac without a shot.

From British Landing M185 continues to skirt the island as a level route, passing the trailhead to Lake Shore Nature Trail at mile 5.5. Take time to hike this short trail in the spring and early summer as it features a profusion of wildflowers, including the endangered yellow lady slipper orchid. At mile 7.5, M185 passes beneath Arch Rock, the most famous limestone formation on the island. A long stairway of 192 steps leads from the road up the steep bluff to an observation area, where you can look through the 50-foot wide arch to Lake Huron.

From Arch Rock you are less than a mile from the downtown area and all those fudge shops.

RIDE GUIDE

★   0.0 From the ferry docks downtown turn left onto Huron Street which becomes M185 (Lake Shore Road).

    3.5 British Landing.

    5.5 Lake Shore Nature Trail.

    7.5 Arch Rock.

    8.4 Downtown area. End of ride.

Calumet Loop
Submitted by Dan Dalquist

This ride leads through a wonderfully scenic area encompassing some of the oldest communities in Michigan. The towns emerged early in the twentieth century, during an era when the region served as a primary producer of copper in the United States.

Type of ride: road bike
Starting point: Hancock City Beach parking lot
Finishing point: same
Distance: 34.2 miles
Level of difficulty: moderate
General terrain: rolling to hilly, over smooth pavement
Traffic conditions: moderate; most roads have shoulders
Estimated riding time: 2 to 3 hours

Great Sand Bay (photo by: Dan Dalquist)

Best season/time of day to ride: June through September, any day of the week.

Points of interest: scenic views of Lake Superior; Keweenaw National Historic Park, one of the newest national parks in the country

Accommodations and services: campgrounds, groceries, restaurants, motels, and bike services available along the route; parking available at the Hancock City Beach

Supplemental maps or other information: available at the Keweenaw Tourism Council office at 326 Shelden Avenue in Houghton; the Keweenaw National Historic Park's guide to a walking tour through the historic business district of Calumet also available at the Tourism Council office

GETTING THERE

Follow US 41 north through the Upper Peninsula city of Houghton, crossing the Portage Lift Bridge into Hancock. Pass through downtown Hancock to the stop sign near the Citgo service station and continue straight onto M203 for 1.3 miles to the Hancock City Beach. Park in the lot.

IN THE SADDLE

From the parking lot, turn left onto M203, heading north along the Portage Lake Ship Canal. The canal effectively makes an island of the Keweenaw Peninsula, which is connected to the mainland only by the Portage Lift Bridge. The road is narrow as it winds along the shoreline to McLain State Park at mile 8.6. Stop here to fill your water bottle and enjoy the view of Lake Superior.

Turn left when leaving the park to continue northeast on M203 toward Calumet. Pass straight through the four-way intersection at 10.2 miles; then begin a 4-mile climb that offers several panoramic vistas of the lake. Especially early in the morning, watch for deer in the fields along the 11.5-mile stretch.

At 14.5 miles, there is a sign announcing distant Isle Royale National Park, which on a clear day is visible across the lake. Enter the Calumet village limits at 16.2 miles and turn right onto 6th Street,

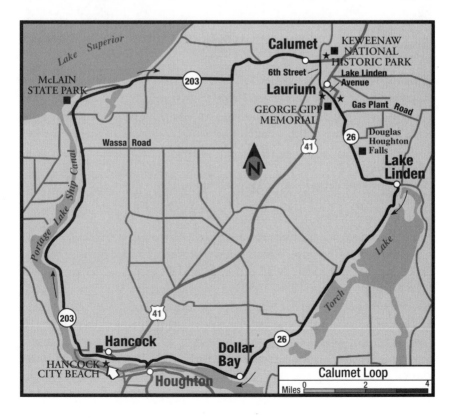

Majestic Lake Superior (photo by: Dan Dalquist)

proceeding south toward US 41. (You will cross Oak Street; the Cross Country Sports bike shop is up this street to your left.) Cross US 41 at mile 17.0, riding onto Lake Linden Avenue; then continue to the stop sign. Here you enter the village of Laurium, home of "The Gipper" of football (and Ronald Reagan) fame. At mile 18.1 is the George Gipp Memorial.

At 19.4 miles, ride onto M26, then continue down the hill toward Lake Linden. At just over a mile into the downhill, watch for a gravel parking area on your left. Here you can pull out and hike the half-mile-long trail to the top of impressive Douglas Houghton Falls.

Continue downhill, passing under a railroad bridge; then take a sharp right to get to the town of Lake Linden, which served as a deep-water port during the 1880–1950 copper-mining era. Ore was delivered to smelters here, where it was converted into ingots and then shipped to factories in Chicago and Detroit. While riding along M26, you will pass through several settlements featuring row after row of identical houses—the sure mark of "company towns." At mile 23.8, note the abandoned dredge along the shoreline.

Proceeding along the gently rolling highway, enter Dollar Bay, the last town before returning to Hancock. As you pedal along, look across Portage River and you can see the Michigan Technological University Headquarters. Soon after you will see the Isle Royale National Park headquarters. Copper once was delivered to the nearby Ripley Smelter by a narrow-gauge railroad, which descended the slopes now encompassed by the Mont Ripley ski hill. From Houghton County Marina, adjacent to the smelter ruins (the complex burned in the early 1960s), you can earn a good view of the impressive Portage Lift Bridge, which connects Hancock and Houghton.

Traffic picks up as you follow US 41 back through Hancock to M203 and the Hancock City Beach, where your ride ends at mile 34.2.

RIDE GUIDE

★   0.0 From the beach parking lot in Hancock, turn left onto M203.

     8.6 McLain State Park.

    10.2 At the four-way stop, continue straight on M203.

★ 16.2 Calumet Village. Turn right onto 6th Street.

★ 17.0 Cross US 41 and ride onto Lake Linden Avenue.

    18.1 George Gipp Memorial.

★ 19.4 Ride onto M26.

    21.7 Lake Linden.

★ 34.2 Follow US 26 to M203 and the Hancock City Beach parking lot. End of ride.

6 Mass City Loop
Submitted by Gary Wisely

On this ride, you will visit the Keweenaw Peninsula, Michigan's Copper Country and the site of aboriginal copper mines.

Type of ride: road bike
Starting point: Baraga State Park
Finishing point: same
Distance: 171 miles
Level of difficulty: easy to moderate
General terrain: flat to gently rolling

Traffic conditions: generally light
Estimated riding time: 3 to 4 days
Best season/time of day to ride: spring through fall
Points of interest: historic mining towns, Portage Lake
Accommodations and services: state parks at Baraga and north of Hancock
Supplemental maps or other information: McLain State Park, (906) 482-0278; Teepee Lake Campground, 8 miles south of Kenton on County Road FH16, (906) 852-3500; Baraga State Park, 1 mile south of Baraga on US 41, (906) 353-6558; Twin Lakes State Park, 3 miles north of Winona on SR26, (906) 288-3321

GETTING THERE

Baraga is in the far northwestern portion of Michigan's Upper Peninsula, bordering L'Anse Bay. From Ironwood, on the Wisconsin/Michigan border, follow M28 (and a 4-mile section of US 141) for 88 miles east to the junction with US 41, northeast of Covington. Turn left onto US 41 and travel 11 miles north toward Baraga. Baraga State Park is 1 mile south of Baraga on US 41.

IN THE SADDLE

This tour will take you through what is sometimes called "Michigan's Treasure Chest" but is more commonly referred to as "Copper Country." Over the years, the area has produced in excess of ten billion pounds of copper. Copper abounds in numerous deposits contained in a series of ancient northward-tilted lava flows and conglomerates. The ore bodies extend for thousands of feet horizontally and have been mined to depths of more than a mile vertically. They dip downward to the north under Lake Superior and emerge again on Isle Royale and the north shore of Lake Superior.

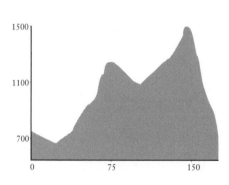

Thousands of years before the arrival of the French, Native Americans worked the surface deposits extensively. From old Indian pits—some of them 500

Spectacular Canyon Falls and Gorge (photo by: Jim DuFresne)

feet in length—tons of pure copper and some silver were laboriously extracted through the use of primitive hand tools. The mystery surrounding this early copper mining is what was done with the metal. Indian artifacts show no evidence that the residents of this area were skilled in working metals. Some scholars believe that the copper was used for trading purposes. You will pass near some of these ancient mines in the scarred landscape just north of Mass City.

From Baraga State Park, turn left onto US 41 and ride north toward the twin lake cities of Hancock and Houghton. Baraga is a bayshore village named in honor of Father Frederick Baraga, who founded a mission at nearby Assinins in 1843. Father Baraga compiled a grammar and dictionary of the difficult Ojibway language so that he might better communicate with the tribes he had come to teach.

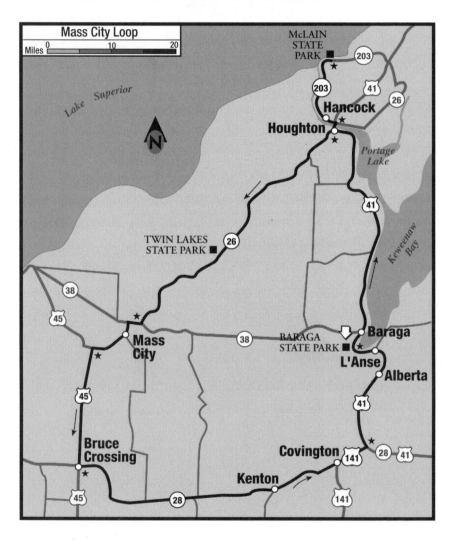

At 29 miles, you will enter Houghton, which lies (as does its sister city Hancock) on shelves of land that rise sharply from the shore of narrow Portage Lake. Founded in 1852, Houghton owes its growth and wealth to the copper industry. It makes sense that the Michigan College of Mining (now Michigan Technological University) was established here; given the surrounding environment, the college is unusually well-prepared to give practical training to students.

Portage Lake extends from Keweenaw Bay northward for 21 miles, nearly cutting in two the 23-mile-wide peninsula. A 2-mile canal dredged by private interests and later taken over by the federal government completed what nature had left unfinished. The canal, from the head of Portage Lake to the Lake Superior shore, makes the upper part of Keweenaw Peninsula an actual island.

Hancock, on the north shore of Portage Lake, was named for the patriot John Hancock and owes its growth and development to copper mining. In 1848, the Quincy Copper Mine opened here and subsequently became one of the leading copper producers of the Marquette Range. The mine, an inclined shaft, had ninety-three levels cut into the rock at regular intervals of about 100 feet. The ore was brought to the surface by "skips," platforms that worked in balance—one rose as the other descended. Each skip weighed approximately 5 tons and could carry about 8 tons of ore when fully loaded. These loaded skips were hoisted at the rate of 3,000 feet per minute; the shaft cables were more than 2 miles in length, wrapped on a drum 30 feet in diameter.

Many of the buildings in Houghton and Hancock are built of native red sandstone. The quarry where the stone was cut, at the eastern entrance to the Keweenaw waterway, about 20 miles southeast of Houghton, was closed in the late nineteenth century. At one time, it was the largest sandstone quarry in the country.

Departing these twin cities, you will turn left onto M203 for the 12-mile journey north to McLain State Park (assuming you will use this park for an overnight stop). To continue the loop, return to Hancock and Houghton via the same route. Arriving once more in Houghton, turn right onto US 41/M26.

South of Houghton, the route continues along the copper-bearing strip. The elevation of the range here affords several wide views of the Keweenaw waterway and the copper country. Between 1855 and 1870, more than a hundred locations were prospected south of Portage Lake.

Many of these penetrated rich lodes, becoming copper bonanzas, but many claims never paid out. There was a huge boom in copper between 1875 and the First World War, but in the post-war decade, other deposits (notably in Montana and South America) were discovered, and the price of copper dropped precipitously.

At mile 77, you will reach the entrance to Twin Lakes State Park. If you did not elect to travel north to McLain State Park, this will make a good overnight stop during your ride (your mileage from Baraga State Park to Twin Lakes, minus the out-and-back ride to McLain State Park, would be approximately 53 miles).

After a jog onto M38 and back to M26, turn left onto the busier US 45 at Mass City. This one-time lumbering village turned to mining and, after the closing of its numerous mines, to dairying. A local cheese factory specializes in Italian-style cheeses. Throughout the hills to the north are great piles of rock, reminders of the mining activity of bygone days. Here you also can see the remains of the ancient copper mines of the early Native Americans.

At Bruce Crossing, turn left onto M28, toward Kenton and Watton. Just west of Watton, M28 crosses the eastern boundary of the Ottawa National Forest at the Lac Vieux Desert Trail. This is an ancient Indian pathway between Burnt Plains and Lac Vieux Desert. At Covington, US 141 joins the route briefly; 5 miles later, bear left to remain on US 41.

Four miles south of L'Anse, you will pass the planned community of Alberta, built by Henry Ford in 1936 as part of an experiment in self-sustaining communities. The original plan called for the settlement of thirty selected families, who were to farm lands cleared in the forest and work at a sawmill in the village. At the time of its settlement, surrounded as it was by miles of unbroken timber and many miles from any other settlement, visitors described it as almost eerie to come upon a completely new village equipped with a well-planned water and sewage system, electricity, boulevard lights, a church, a school, and a fire department.

You will cycle around the southern tip of L'Anse Bay (*l'anse* means "the bay" in French). This small, well-sheltered area was a popular campground for French explorers, trappers, and missionaries on their westward journeys. It signals the end of your journey, which ends back at Baraga State Park.

RIDE GUIDE

★   0.0 From Baraga State Park, ride north on US 41.
      1.0 Baraga.
★ 29.0 Houghton. Turn right to follow US 41/M26.
★ 30.0 Turn left onto M203 North.
★ 42.0 McLain State Park. Turn around and ride back the way that
      you came on M203.
★ 54.0 Houghton. Turn right onto US 41/M26.
      55.0 Continue south on M26. US 41 leaves the route.
      77.0 Twin Lakes State Park.
★ 97.0 Turn right onto M38 and then left onto M26.
★ 102.0 Turn left onto US 45.
★ 116.0 Turn left onto M28.
      133.0 Kenton.
      151.0 Covington. US 141 joins route.
★ 155.0 Bear left to follow US 41.
      167.0 L'Anse.
      171.0 Baraga State Park. End of ride.

 Cedarville Shuffle

Submitted by John Stevens

This is a beautiful 22-mile ride along the Lake Huron shore—with lots of sand beaches and coniferous forests—taking you to De Tour on the southeastern tip of the Upper Peninsula.

Type of ride: road bike
Starting point: M134 in Cedarville
Finishing point: De Tour Village
Distance: 22 miles
Level of difficulty: moderate
General terrain: rolling
Traffic conditions: moderate
Estimated riding time: 2 to 4 hours
Best season/time of day to ride: spring through fall

Points of interest: resort villages along Lake Huron
Accommodations and services: restaurants and restrooms available along the route; hotels and meals available in Cedarville and De Tour
Supplemental maps or other information: none

GETTING THERE
From the Mackinac Bridge, drive north on I-75 for 16 miles to the junction with M134. Turn east (right) onto M134 and drive 17 miles to Cedarville. Park in the vicinity of Les Cheneaux Historical Museum, at the junction of Meridian Road and M134.

IN THE SADDLE
Cedarville was an early Michigan lumbering community and was named for its chief product during those heady days when the supply of lumber was considered inexhaustible. Depart Cedarville to the east on M134. The road is flat with rolling hills and glacial valleys but still relatively easy to navigate.

At 6 miles is Bush Bay, which offers a turnout spot that makes a good place to enjoy a snack. You may from this viewpoint see ore freighters loading dolomite rock at Port Dolomite, just across the bay. In another

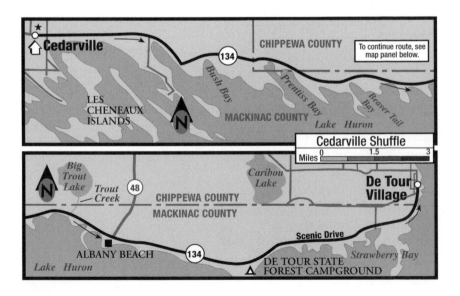

2.5 miles you will reach Prentiss Bay, the location of a large lumber camp that was converted in this century to a religious camp. In another 1.8 miles is Beaver Tail Bay. A gravel road leads down to the lake for a short side trip.

The area through which you are riding is called Les Cheneaux, French for "the channels." This is an archipelago formed by glacial action during the Ice Age. The glacier moved from northwest to southeast, scouring out grooves as it moved—deep grooves, perhaps 100 to 200 feet in some places. Offshore, this action formed islands with intervening channels: hence, the name *Les Cheneaux*. Just offshore of Cedarville lie the thirty-five islands forming Les Cheneaux Islands.

Continue on M134 past Trout Creek and Albany Creek to the intersection with M48. Continue straight ahead, past Albany Beach, referred to locally as "Long Beach." This is a lovely stretch of sandy shore and low dunes where many people come to swim, lounge in the sun, and play volleyball. A mile from the parking area on Albany Beach is a roadside park that is another nice place to take a break—there are picnic tables and restrooms, and water is available.

In 1.2 miles from the roadside park is the De Tour State Forest Campground on Lake Huron. Continue past the campground and Strawberry Bay to the sign for the De Tour Village limits (the village itself isn't evident for another 2 miles). The town's name refers to the sharp turn that ships had to make to enter the St. Mary's River, through which all ships must pass on their way to Sault Ste. Marie. Prior to its role as a shipping lane marker, the site of De Tour Village was a trading post that attracted a semi-permanent population of as many as 3,000 Native Americans.

De Tour Village is the end of the route, but from here you can take a side trip to Drummond Island. The island has a variety of blacktop, gravel, and dirt roads, and it is best known as an uninhabited retreat for hunters and fishers. It has a small shopping center at Four Corners and a virtual ghost town at Johnswood. Island traffic is light but tends to move quite fast.

RIDE GUIDE

★   0.0 From Cedarville, ride east on M134.
6.0 Bush Bay.
8.5 Prentiss Bay.

10.3 Beaver Tail Bay.
14.1 Trout Creek.
16.3 Albany Beach.
17.5 De Tour State Forest Campground.
19.7 Strawberry Bay.
21.7 De Tour Village. Turn right to continue on M134.
22.0 End of ride.

Escanaba Explorer
Submitted by Gary Wisely

On this ride, you will tour several of the historic mining towns of the Marquette Range, well known for its iron ore deposits.

Type of ride: road bike
Starting point: Rapid River
Finishing point: same
Distance: 210 miles
Level of difficulty: easy to moderate
General terrain: flat to gently rolling
Traffic conditions: mostly lightly traveled roads; some busier sections on US highways
Estimated riding time: 3 to 5 days
Best season/time of day to ride: spring to fall
Points of interest: historic iron ore mining operations
Accommodations and services: state parks and private campgrounds; many towns along the way offer full services
Supplemental maps or other information: Vagabond Resort and Campground, 2.5 miles east of Rapid River on US 2, 3 miles south on County Road 513T, (906) 474-6122; Escanaba River State Forest Campground, 1 mile southeast of Little Lake on M35, (906) 786-2351; Copper County State Forest Campground, 4 miles west of Channing via Campground Road, (906) 353-6651; Norway Lake County Park, 3.5 miles southwest of Ralph on County Road 581, at southeast end of Norway Lake

GETTING THERE

Cross onto the Upper Peninsula via the Mackinac Bridge and at St. Ignace take the US 2-West exit. Follow US 2 for 125 miles until you are 2 miles east of Rapid River. Turn left (south) onto County Road 513T for 3 miles to Vagabond Resort and Campground. (An alternate campground is Whitefish Hill Campground and Trailer Park, 1 mile east of Rapid River on the south side of US 2.)

IN THE SADDLE

Your ride begins at the Vagabond Resort and Campground. You will ride north on County Road 513T and then turn left onto US 2. This will take you into Rapid River, located where the Whitefish River empties into Little Bay De Noc. Three miles farther on, turn right onto County Road 186. In another 5 miles, you will reach M35. Turn right onto M35 toward Rock.

The village of Rock was a stop on the Marquette stagecoach route until 1865, when the Chicago & Northwestern Railway began operations. The first permanent settlers arrived about 1864 to cut maple forests for the charcoal kilns. When the panic of 1873 closed most of the ovens, the populace turned to farming and large-scale poultry raising. Lumbering regained importance after the turn of the century. Many of the early settlers in these towns were Finnish.

At 42 miles, you will reach Little Lake. Three miles farther is Gwinn, which began as a model community built in 1907 by the Cleveland Cliffs Iron Company for its employees. Situated on the East Branch of the Escanaba River, the lots and houses were sold to the employees at cost, and the company erected the schools, hospitals, and other public buildings. Most of the villages along this section of road are small and quiet now, but during the late nineteenth century they were thriving communities whose inhabitants found employment in planing and shingle mills and at charcoal kilns, all shut down long ago. At 64 miles, you will arrive at Palmer, which sits in a hill-locked valley where iron ore mining began during the closing days of the Civil War.

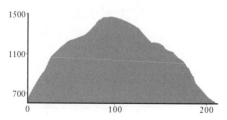

A left turn onto County Road 480 will take you into Negaunee, which is Indian for "pioneer," or "the first," an appropriate name for the first mining city on the Marquette Range, which produced a number of rich iron ore deposits. In 1844, a surveying party discovered the Negaunee site, later named Jackson Hill. Erosion had scoured away the coating of soil over the iron deposits, and the ore could be pried loose with picks. It was then broken up with sledges and moved to the stock piles in horsecars. The mine remained for years a crude quarry because rough forest trails were the only means of shipping the ore to Marquette, 13 miles away. In the winter, the stock piles of ore were transported to Marquette on sleds. About 1,000 tons were moved each winter in this manner.

A tramway to Marquette was completed in 1854. It had wooden rails protected by strips of iron, over which mule cars could haul a four-ton load.

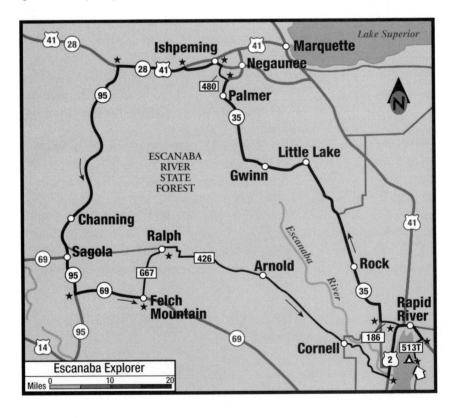

After five years of work, the Iron Mountain Railroad—connecting Ishpeming, Negaunee, and Marquette—was completed in 1857, and iron ore shipments increased from 1,000 tons annually in the 1840s to 135,000 tons in 1871. By the First World War, production was 1,800,000 tons annually. On Iron Street in the western section of Negaunee is a 12-foot pyramid of iron ore blocks, erected by the Jackson Iron Company in 1904 to mark the first discovery of iron ore in the Lake Superior region.

In Negaunee, turn left onto M28/US 41 toward Ishpeming. This mining town takes its name from an Indian word meaning "high grounds" or "heaven." Attracted by the purity of the Marquette Range iron ore, the Cleveland Cliffs Iron Company and the Oliver Mining Company established headquarters in the city, and Henry Ford opened a mine nearby. The second active iron ore mine in the state of Michigan was opened in Ishpeming when it was still little more than a campsite. Because ore deposits were richer and more widely distributed here than elsewhere, Ishpeming for a time outstripped all neighboring cities in production, growth, and wealth.

Continue west on M28/US 41 to the junction with M95. Turn left (south) onto M95. Just to the east of your route as you cross the Michigamme River basin is Republic, which was also called Iron City when it was settled in 1871. In the following year, 11,000 tons of iron ore were shipped from the Republic Mine. Operations continued steadily until the late 1920s. Piles of blue rock still are strewn about the area, evidence of the past mining activities.

M69 joins M95 at Sagola. Continue approximately 5 miles south on M95 to the junction where M69 departs M95 and turn left onto M69.

At Felch Mountain, turn left (north) onto G67/M581. At the crossroads, turn right (east) onto County Road 426. These back roads take you deeper into the Escanaba River State Forest. Escanaba comes from the Ojibway word *eshkonabang*, meaning "land of the red buck." You will cycle through farming and fishing centers, areas once dense with forests of cedar, birch, and poplar and groves of large pine, beeches, and elms that alternated with areas of poor, stony soil.

At 196 miles into the tour, turn left onto US 2, which will return you to Rapid River to close the loop. Turn right (south) onto County Road 513T to return to the starting point of the ride.

There are six state forest campgrounds within easy riding distance of the Escanaba Explorer loop. Amenities at the rustic sites include picnic tables, fire rings, and vault toilets. (photo by: Jim DuFresne)

RIDE GUIDE

★   0.0 From the Vagabond Resort and Campground, ride north on County Road 513T.

★   3.1 Turn left onto US 2.

★   6.0 Turn right onto County Road 186.

★   11.0 Turn right onto M35.

   24.2 Rock.

   42.0 Little Lake.

   64.2 Palmer.

★   70.1 Turn left onto County Road 480.

★   75.3 Turn left onto M28/US 41.

   78.0 Ishpeming. Continue on M28/US 41.

★   81.2 Turn left onto M28/US 41.

★   92.0 Turn left onto M95.

  121.0 Channing.

  125.3 Sagola.

★ 130.0 Turn left onto M69.

★ 143.4 Felch Mountain. Turn left onto G67/M581.

★ 152.0 Ralph. Turn right onto County Road 426.

  168.8 Arnold.

  186.4 Cornell.

★ 196.0 Turn left onto US 2.

  204.0 Rapid River.

★ 210.0 Turn right (south) onto County Road 513T. End of ride.

 9

North Lake Trek
Submitted by Karl Fava

This road bike tour along the shores of Lake Michigan takes you through early lumbering and fishing communities, ending in St. Ignace, Michigan's second oldest community.

Type of ride: road bike
Starting point: Manistique
Finishing point: Star Line ferry dock in St. Ignace
Distance: 89.5 miles

Level of difficulty: moderate
General terrain: generally flat
Traffic conditions: two-lane US highway; traffic very heavy during summer weekends
Estimated riding time: 2 45-mile days or 3 leisurely days
Best season/time of day to ride: spring through fall
Points of interest: St. Ignace, historic fishing and lumbering towns
Accommodations and services: groceries in small towns along the way; see map for campground locations
Supplemental maps or other information: none

GETTING THERE

Follow I-75 North to the Mackinac Bridge and cross onto the Upper Peninsula. Immediately north of the bridge, take the US 2-West exit. Follow US 2 for 89 miles to Manistique, which will provide you with a good preview of your ride. (Or, park in St. Ignace at the ferry terminal and ride this tour in reverse, ending in Manistique.)

IN THE SADDLE

Manistique is situated at the mouth of the river that bears the same name, which comes from a Chippewa word meaning "vermilion." The town started as a lumbering development during the Civil War. It grew to become one of the Upper Peninsula's largest lumber centers, with mills and docks that extended several miles upstream. At the peak of production, the mills had an output of ninety million board feet of pine annually, much of which went to build Chicago and other expanding Midwest cities.

By the turn of the century, the supply of pine was exhausted, and the lumber mills closed. The region's economy became based upon the operation of lime kilns, iron furnaces, hardwood manufacture, paper-making, and commercial fishing. It is also a popular destination for boating, as it provides access to the three hundred lakes and numerous streams within the Lake Superior State Forest.

You depart Manistique on US 2, which you will follow for the entire tour to St. Ignace. At 12 miles is Gulliver, which some of the old-timers still refer to as Whitedale. Blaney Park, which is located just 1 mile off the route at Mile 21, is located on a 22,000-acre tract purchased in 1886 by the Wisconsin Land and Lumber Company. In 1926, when the property had been almost completely logged off, the owners made a resort community of the tract; groups of cottages were built, and old logging roads became riding and hiking trails. Some sections were marked for bird sanctuaries and game preserves.

At 44 miles, you will reach Naubinway, and at 61 miles the small community of Epoufette. Midway between the two communities is a primitive campground at Hog Island Point. There is also a campground just east of Brevort, a fishing village settled in 1884 which became known in the 1880s as "The Warehouse" because of a storage building used by a steamship line running between St. Ignace and Manistique. In the 1880s and 1890s, lumber companies would store up a winter's worth of cut logs at Brevort, awaiting the opening of navigation on Lake Michigan. In the spring, lumberjacks broke the "rollways," and the logs thundered down 100-foot sandhills into the lake, where they were formed into rafts and towed to the mills.

There are several place names derived from French that are important in this area: Gros Cap is French for "big cape" and refers to a blunt-nosed out-thrust of land over which you will cross; Pointe Aux Chenes is French for "point of the oak trees." Gros Cap was a small fishing village founded in 1855 by a Mormon named Cheeseman. Visible 2 miles

Enjoying the famed beach of Lake Michigan near Brevort (photo by: Jim DuFresne)

off Gros Cap is St. Helena Island, at one time a refueling station for wood-burning steamers plying the Straits.

At just under 90 miles, you will enter St. Ignace, the state's second-oldest settlement, lying at the threshold of the Upper Peninsula. Although the first white man, Jean Nicolet, arrived in 1634, followed by trappers seeking riches in the fur business, the town was not founded until 1671 when Father Jacques Marquette built a mission chapel here. In 1679, the explorer La Salle's ship, *The Griffon*, on its way to Green Bay for furs, put in at St. Ignace and then disappeared without a trace somewhere near the Straits on its return journey. Early in the eighteenth century, fishers arrived from Canada, on the heels of the fur traders, and clung tenaciously to the peninsula, setting their nets for whitefish and trout. St. Ignace was incorporated as a village in 1882. The city's favored location as the entry port to the Upper Peninsula has helped it maintain a steady growth. Today, in addition to the continued fishing, the city welcomes thousands of tourists who wish to explore Mackinac Island and the Upper Peninsula. The bridge from the mainland replaced ferry service in 1952.

As you enter St. Ignace, bear left to remain on US 2/State Street (Ferry Street bears to the right). Your ride ends at the docks of the Star Line Ferry in St. Ignace.

RIDE GUIDE

★   0.0 From the east end of Manistique, ride east on US 2.
12.0 Gulliver.
21.1 Blaney Park.
24.2 Enter Schoolhouse County.
38.6 Junction with M117. Continue on US 2.
44.4 Naubinway.
60.9 Epoufette.
67.5 Brevort.
89.5 St. Ignace.
★ 90.1 At fork, bear left to stay on State Street.
89.5 Star Line Ferry dock. End of ride.

St. Ignace Trek
Submitted by John Stevens

The St. Ignace Trek is a 33-mile ride, mostly through lovely forests of pine, cedar, and hemlock.

Type of ride: road bike
Starting point: Arnold's Dock #1 in St. Ignace
Finishing point: Cedarville
Distance: 32.5 miles
Level of difficulty: moderate
General terrain: gently rolling; some hills
Traffic conditions: heavier on M134 during the tourist season
Estimated riding time: 3 hours
Best season/time of day to ride: spring through fall
Points of interest: St. Ignace museums; dock areas in small towns
Accommodations and services: all services at St. Ignace and Cedarville
Supplemental maps or other information: none

GETTING THERE

Follow I-75 north to the Mackinac Bridge. Shortly after crossing the bridge, take the St. Ignace exit to the right. Turn right onto US 2 at the top of the hill. This east-west road turns into State Street in the business district of St. Ignace and follows the waterfront. Watch for Arnold's Dock (also the departure point for the Mackinac Island Tour, Ride 4). There are large parking lots in the vicinity, primarily for those using the ferry boats to the various Lake Huron islands.

IN THE SADDLE

St. Ignace was the site of an early French Jesuit Mission to the Ottawas and Chippewas. Established in 1671, the first mission was moved to the south shoreline of the Straits when Fort Michilimackinac was built on the site of what is today Mackinaw City. To avoid confusion, you might want to note that this local place name has two spellings—*Mackinac* and *Mackinaw* are both pronounced Mac-i-naw.

From the Arnold's Dock parking area in St. Ignace, follow State Street (US 2 North) to the exit for Evergreen Shores and the Mackinac Trail (Old US 2), which follows the Lake Huron shoreline to Cedarville. Mackinac Trail is the old highway between St. Ignace and Sault Ste. Marie. (The latter is pronounced "Soo Saint Marie" and is commonly referred to in the area as simply "the Soo.")

Your route traverses pine, cedar, and hemlock forest for most of its length. You will also notice the outcroppings of limestone, in some places high enough to appear as miniature mountain ridges. This is the northern shoreline of the ancient Michigan Basin, left from a sea that covered most of Michigan and parts of Illinois, Wisconsin, Ohio, Kentucky, Indiana, and eastern Ontario. The fossilized skeletons of the corals and shellfish built up over the eons into the shoreline of this sea. They remain today as a rocky ridge of limestone still outlining the Michigan Basin. On nearby Drummond Island, and in other locations, there are quarries where the limestone is cut and shaped for use as a building material. All of the villages along the route include waterfront areas with docks for shipping and yachting.

Continue to the junction of the Mackinac Trail with M134, also known as Les Cheneaux Highway. The area through which you are riding is often called Les Cheneaux, which is French for "the channels"

The gravesite of Father Marquette in St. Ignace (photo by: Jim DuFresne)

and refers to the islands and channels formed offshore by glacial action during the Ice Age.

Turn right onto M134 and follow the road (known here as North Huron Shore Drive) across low hills to Hessel, passing the red waters of Pine River and Nunn's Creek. Traffic is heavier during the tourist season, and the route is used by many bicyclists as well. From Hessel, continue east on M134 into Cedarville. This early lumbering community—busy when there was an "endless" supply of cedar in the region—now depends upon the traffic of visitors to Les Cheneaux Islands, a grouping of thirty-five islands just offshore. The islands protect the channels between them from the more violent wave action of Lake Huron, and so motor boating is a popular activity here.

RIDE GUIDE
- ★ 0.0 From Arnold's Dock #1 in St. Ignace, ride north on State Street/US 2.
- ★ 3.9 Turn right onto Mackinac Trail/County Road H63.
- 12.9 Carp River Campground.

★ 15.5 Turn right onto M134.
16.6 Bear right to continue on M134.
21.8 Cross Nunn's Creek.
28.7 Hessel.
★ 32.3 Turn right onto M134/M129.
32.5 Cedarville. End of ride.

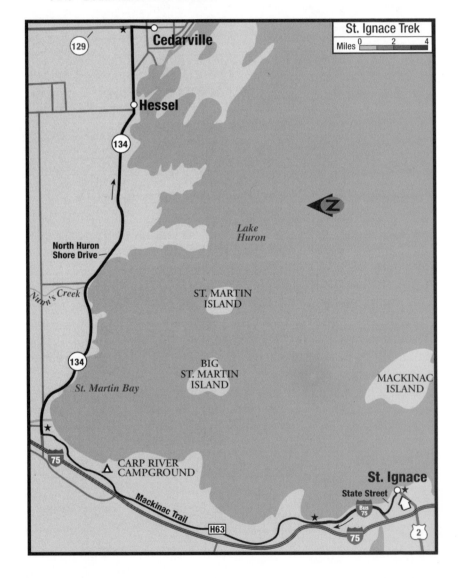

Region 2:
North Lakes

A well-marked trail crossing (photo by: Laurie McPhillips)

Cadillac Pathway

Submitted by Michael McPhillips

The Cadillac Pathway is a multi-looped, single-track trail in the Père Marquette State Forest. Ride lengths vary from 1.5 miles to 10 miles or longer, with loops on the eastern side more accommodating to young or novice riders.

Type of ride: mountain bike
Starting point: Cadillac Pathway trailhead
Finishing point: same
Distance: varies with loop—1.5 to 10 miles or more
Level of difficulty: easy to moderate
General terrain: varies with route; includes several stretches of long hills on varied surfaces; well-maintained trail
Traffic conditions: light
Estimated riding time: at least 1 hour, more time for longer loops
Best season/time of day to ride: weekdays in late spring and early fall
Points of interest: trees, Clam River
Accommodations and services: trail maps permanently posted at twelve points along path
Supplemental maps or other information: Cadillac Area Visitors Center, 122 West Chapin, Cadillac, MI 49601, (616) 775-9776; Père Marquette State Forest District Office, 8015 South Mackinaw Trail (US 131), Cadillac, MI 49601, (616) 775-9727

GETTING THERE

From Grand Rapids, take US 131 north through Cadillac to Boon Road (34 Mile Road). Turn east on Boon Road and continue for 3.5 miles until the road makes a hard curve to the left where it joins Seeley Road. The parking lot is a short distance farther on the right. A sign marks the Cadillac Pathway on the side of the road.

IN THE SADDLE

Cadillac (both the town and the car) were named for Antoine de la Mothe Cadillac, the founder of Detroit. The town was initially settled in 1871 by timber speculators, and the village was incorporated in 1877.

Your ride begins at Trail Marker 1 at the trailhead. At Marker 4,

A relaxing spot along the Cadillac Pathway (photo by: Laurie McPhillips)

the trail begins a long uphill climb. There are several big hills in this section, making it tougher than the others. At Marker 8 is an intersection and park benches. To return to the parking lot, turn left and follow the trail for 1.1 miles. The longer route, marked by many hills, continues on the original trail to Marker 9. The trail surface is rougher, with more areas of sand and gravel. Some sections of steep gravel also have a surface for bikes to increase traction and decrease erosion. After Marker 9, the hills aren't as numerous or as big.

Another option to return to the parking lot is available at Marker 10. Turn off for Marker 11 and go a short distance to the trail's end at a school parking lot. From the lot, turn right onto 13th Street, then right at the first intersection. Another mile brings the route to Boon Road. Turn right again and bike the last 3.5 miles back to your starting point.

To ride out the rest of the trail, ride from Marker 10 to Marker 12, a section of many downgrades. The route continues past Marker 12 to Marker 8. From Marker 8, head east toward Marker 5. This section is

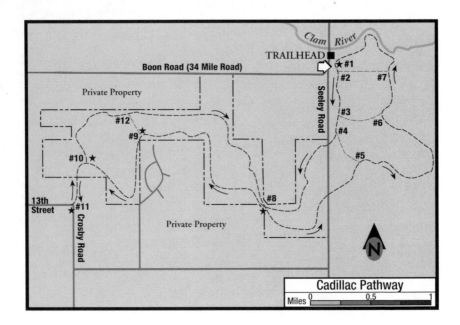

similar to the last one, only with fewer hills. A stop sign on the way to Marker 5 indicates where the route crosses Seeley Road. Continue on to Marker 6 and 7 as the trail gets narrower due to encroachment by the surrounding trees. Marker 7 indicates the beginning of the last leg. Here the trail becomes level and winds through trees to a clearing along the Clam River. The trail ends back at the parking area.

RIDE GUIDE

★   0.0 From the parking lot at the trailhead, ride past Trail Marker 1 in the southeast corner of the parking area.

0.1 At Marker 2, continue straight.

0.5 At Marker 3, continue straight.

0.7 At Marker 4, continue straight.

★   1.6 At Marker 8, bear to the left toward Marker 9.

★   2.9 At Marker 9, turn left.

★   3.6 At Marker 10, turn left.

★   3.9 At Marker 11, turn around.

4.2 At Marker 10, continue straight.
4.9 At Marker 12, continue straight.
6.5 At Marker 8, continue straight.
7.6 At Marker 5, continue straight.
9.0 At Marker 6, continue straight.
9.4 At Marker 7, continue straight.
10.2 Parking lot. End of ride.

Torch Lake Loop
Submitted by Thomas Rea

This 51-mile loop takes you clockwise around very scenic Torch Lake, just east of Grand Traverse Bay.

Type of ride: road bike
Starting point: Alden
Finishing point: same
Distance: 51.1 miles
Level of difficulty: easy to moderate
General terrain: flat with some gentle hills climbing away from the shoreline
Traffic conditions: low traffic volumes except for two brief sections of US 31
Estimated riding time: 5 to 6 hours
Best season/time of day to ride: spring through late fall
Points of interest: nonstop scenery at Torch Lake; Grand Traverse Bay
Accommodations and services: few along route; bring your own food and water
Supplemental maps or other information: none

GETTING THERE
From Traverse City, take US 31 east for 35 miles to its junction with M88. Turn right onto M88 and travel east 1 mile to the junction with M593/East Torch Lake Drive. Drive 20 miles south to the town of Alden and park.

IN THE SADDLE

This clockwise loop ride around 21-mile-long Torch Lake begins and ends in the small town of Alden, located on the southeast shore of the lake. Depart Alden on East Torch Lake Drive (M593). As you come around the southernmost shore, M593 becomes Crystal Beach Road. At just under 5 miles, you will turn right onto West Shore Drive.

Torch Lake was named for the local Indians' practice of spearing fish in the lake at night by torchlight. It is quite a beautiful lake: the white sand beaches and the dark green trees on its banks make a lovely setting for its translucent, spring-fed waters. The hues of the water vary widely: Close to the shore, the waters are the palest blue, but in the center where the lake reaches a depth of 300 feet, the waters change to a cobalt blue that is almost purple.

The shoreline road does not completely circumnavigate the lake, so you will have to make a few turns as you head north along the western shore. At 7.5 miles, just past Deepwater Point, turn left onto Hickin Road and then, in a half-mile, turn right onto Western Road. West Shore Drive does continue beyond the junction with Hickin Road, but you will find yourself at a dead end if you follow it.

At 10.4 miles, turn left off Western Road onto Bussa Road and head west to its intersection with Cherry Avenue. Turn right onto Cherry Avenue, which will lead you around the northeast shore of Elk Lake. Across this lake is the town of Elk Rapids, settled in 1852 around a sawmill powered by the Elk River. A charcoal iron furnace utilized the timber resources of the region for many years.

At 13.5 miles, turn right off Cherry Avenue onto Cairn Highway/ US 31 for a short jog (approximately 0.2 mile) to the intersection with Indian Road. Watch for higher traffic volumes on Cairn Highway. Turn right onto Indian Road and head back toward the Torch Lake shoreline.

Rejoin the western shoreline road, now called West Torch Lake Drive, at mile 16.2. Turn left onto West Torch Lake Drive and continue north. At 24.8 miles, turn left onto Barnes Road for another brief jog away from the lakeshore. One mile later, take a right onto Cairn Highway, which leads to the north end of the lake. (Again, expect higher traffic volumes here.) Barnes County Park is located just west of the junction of the Cairn Highway (US 31) and M88. You are now about halfway finished with the ride, so this narrow spit of land between Torch Lake

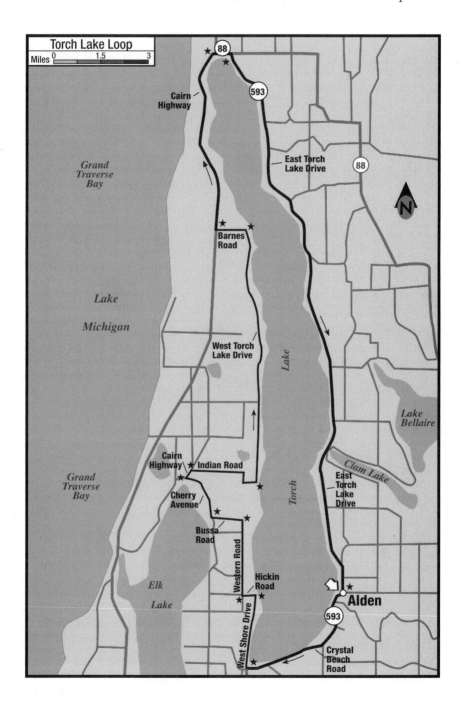

and the waters of Lake Michigan's Grand Traverse Bay makes a good place for lunch and a breather. The bay was named by the French voyageurs who referred to their trip across it as *le grande traversée*, French for "the great crossing."

To continue your ride, turn right off Cairn Highway onto M88, riding east across the northern shore of Torch Lake. In just less than a mile, at mile 32, turn right onto East Torch Lake Drive/M593.

The return section of your route hugs the shoreline all the way back to Alden, which makes tour directions much easier to follow. Enjoy.

RIDE GUIDE

★   0.0 From Alden, ride south on East Torch Lake Drive (M593).
★   4.9 Turn right onto West Shore Drive.
★   7.5 Turn left onto Hickin Road.
★   8.0 Turn right onto Western Road.
★   10.4 Turn left onto Bussa Road.
★   11.5 Turn right onto Cherry Avenue.
★   13.5 Turn right onto Cairn Highway.
★   13.7 Turn right onto Indian Road.
★   16.2 Turn left onto West Torch Lake Drive.
★   24.8 Turn left onto Barnes Road.
★   25.8 Turn right onto Cairn Highway (US 31).
★   31.3 Turn right onto M88.
★   32.0 Turn right onto East Torch Lake Drive/M593.
    51.1 Alden. End of ride.

Mio Ride

13

Submitted by Gary Wisely

This is a fairly easy 80-mile ride through the Huron National Forest and the Au Sable State Forest, partially along the Au Sable River, a popular stream for trout fishing.

Type of ride: road bike
Starting point: Mio
Finishing point: same

Distance: 80.5 miles
Level of difficulty: easy
General terrain: flat to gently rolling
Traffic conditions: generally light; medium traffic but good shoulders on M72
Estimated riding time: 1 day for a hard ride or 2 days for a leisurely ride
Best season/time of day to ride: late spring to late fall
Points of interest: Au Sable River; Kirtland warbler nesting sites (in spring)
Accommodations and services: Au Sable State Forest, Mio Pond, 3 miles west of Mio on M33 and Popps Road, (517) 826-3211; Alcona Park–East Primitive Area, 4 miles west of Glennie and M65, 1.5 miles north on Au Sable Road, (517) 735-3881; U.S. Forest Service campgrounds at McCollum Lake and Parmalee Bridge
Supplemental maps or other information: none

GETTING THERE
From southern Michigan take I-75 to exit 202 at Alger; then take M33 north for 38 miles to Mio. From northern Michigan take I-75 south, exit at Grayling (exit 256), and turn east on M72. Follow M72 for 32 miles to Mio.

IN THE SADDLE
Surrounded by the Huron and Au Sable forests, and with the Au Sable River (a popular trout stream) at its front door, Mio is a logical departure point for many fishing and canoeing expeditions. The region is also known by birders because each spring the rare Kirtland warbler nests in protected areas just south of Mio at Mack Lake.

Begin at Mio Pond and ride north on Gerber Road. There are several quick turns: at 1 mile, turn right onto Popps Road; at just over 2 miles, turn left onto M33; and, in another mile, turn right onto County Road 600 (McKinley Road).

Follow County Road 600, which will have several names before you leave it. At 8 miles into your ride, you will pass a T intersection with County Road 601 (Abbe Road); continue straight on County Road 600. Approximately 3 miles later, ride onto Old State Road, as 600 splits, and the right-hand branch drops southeast to the small burgh of McKinley.

The Huron National Forest extends over nearly 965,000 acres in the northern part of the Lower Peninsula. The Au Sable River, just to

Setting up camp (photo by: Gary Wisely)

the south of your present position, was once heavily used as a waterway for floating logs from the surrounding forests to the sawmills at East Tawas and Oscoda. Today, the river provides hydroelectric power from the dams along its course (you passed one leaving Mio).

At just over 19 miles, bear right off County Road 600 onto Au Sable Road. Turn left onto Aspen Alley Road. Within 3 miles, you will come to an intersection with M65; this will be indicated on some signs as De Jarlais Road. Turn left (northeast) onto M65. This will take you to Curran.

Continue riding north on M65. At 33.7 miles, you will reach the intersection with McCollum Lake Road (the same road is called Crowell Road to the right, or east). Turn left (west) onto McCollum Lake Road. You will arrive at the U.S. Forest Service campground at McCollum Lake at the 40-mile point in the ride.

Leaving McCollum Lake, follow McCollum Lake Road (also marked County Road 607) south for approximately 4.5 miles to the junction with M72. Turn right (west) onto M72. This is locally marked in the vicinity of Fairview as Miller Road.

At 57.6 miles, ride straight onto County Road 608 (still Miller Road). Two miles later, you will cross the intersection with Galbraith Road. Continue west until the 65.5 mile point, where you intersect

County Road 489. Turn left (south) onto County Road 489. At 68.3 miles, turn left (east) onto Cherry Creek Road/County Road 606.

At 77.5 miles, turn right onto M33/M72, near the Mio Airport. In 1 mile, turn right onto Popps Road and then left onto Gerber Road. This will return you to your starting point.

RIDE GUIDE

★   0.0 From Mio Pond in Au Sable State Forest, ride north on Gerber Road.

★   1.0 Turn right onto Popps Road.

★   2.1 Turn left onto M33.

★   3.1 Turn right onto County Road 600 (McKinley Road).

    8.0 Intersect County Road 601 (Abbe Road).

★ 19.2 Bear right onto Au Sable Road.

★ 22.1 Bear left onto Aspen Alley Road.

   26.9 Ride onto M65 North.

   27.9 Curran.

   28.8 Intersect M72/Miller Road. Continue straight on M65.

★ 33.7 Turn left onto McCollum Lake Road.

   39.7 U.S. Forest Service campground. Continue straight on McCollum Lake Road (County Road 607).

★ 44.6 Turn right onto M72.

   53.9 Fairview. Continue straight on M72/M33.

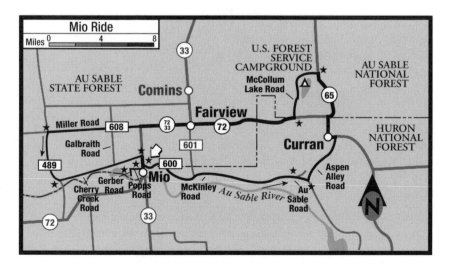

One of the Upper Peninsula's many backroads (photo by: Gary Wisely)

57.6 Ride straight onto County Road 608 (Miller Road).
59.6 Intersect Galbraith Road.
★ 65.5 Turn left onto County Road 489 (Red Oak Road).
★ 68.3 Turn left onto Cherry Creek Road.
74.3 Intersect County Road 609 (Galbraith Road).
★ 77.5 Turn right onto M33/M72.
★ 78.5 Turn right onto Popps Road.
★ 79.5 Turn left onto Gerber Road.
80.5 End of ride.

Shingle Mill Pathway
Submitted by Alan Fark

This is a relatively short loop ride that makes a great excursion for the active family that wants to bicycle without concern for car traffic. More accomplished cyclists will enjoy the scenery and the forest experience.

Type of ride: mountain bike
Starting point: Pigeon Bridge Campground
Finishing point: same
Distance: 6.1 miles
Level of difficulty: moderate
General terrain: gently rolling
Traffic conditions: none (off-road trails)
Estimated riding time: 1 hour
Best season/time of day to ride: May through October
Points of interest: sink holes and forest scenery
Accommodations and services: none
Supplemental maps or other information: Mackinaw State Forest
    Headquarters, Michigan Department of Natural Resources, has
    maps and additional information for the Pigeon River: Call (517)
    983-4101.

GETTING THERE
The Shingle Mill Pathway is located near Vanderbilt, Michigan. From
I-75 north of Gaylord take exit 290. Proceed east on Sturgeon Valley
Road for approximately 10 miles. Turn left after crossing the Pigeon
River to enter the parking lot at the trailhead to the Shingle Mill Path-
way. Parking is ample and additional maps are available here.

IN THE SADDLE
From the parking area, ride across Sturgeon Valley Road and onto the
Shingle Mill Pathway. You will be riding on a closed loop pathway
through some varied northern Michigan topography in the Mackinaw
State Forest. There is one 120-foot climb to an overlook with excellent
vistas.

At just under a mile into the ride, bear right to remain on the path.
The Forest Area Headquarters is located at the 2.2-mile point in the
ride. Just after you pass Pigeon River Campground, turn left onto the
6 Mile Loop trail; then cross Pigeon Bridge Road. Just prior to the end
of the ride, you will turn left onto Sturgeon Valley Road.

The pathway includes boardwalks over several swampy sections, as
well as good single-track sections through pine forests. You also will pass
several glacial sinkholes and kettle lakes. Many of the sinkholes aver-
age 12 acres in size. A few are dry, but others are filled with deep, cold,

clear spring water. The largest sinkhole is just north of the loop and is called Ford Lake. Others have names, such as the Devil's Soup Bowl and Paul Bunyan's Punch Bowl.

Pigeon River Campground is located at the 3-mile point, approximately halfway around the loop, so you could make an overnight tour out of the loop if you wish.

RIDE GUIDE

★   0.0 From the Pigeon Bridge Campground parking lot, ride across Sturgeon Valley Road onto the Shingle Mill Pathway.

★   0.8 Bear right to continue on trail.

  2.2 Forest Area Headquarters.

  3.0 Pigeon River Campground.

  3.1 Cross Pigeon Bridge Road.

★   3.4 Turn left onto the 6 Mile Loop trail and then cross Pigeon Bridge Road.

★   5.9 Turn left onto Sturgeon Valley Road.

  6.1 Parking lot. End of ride.

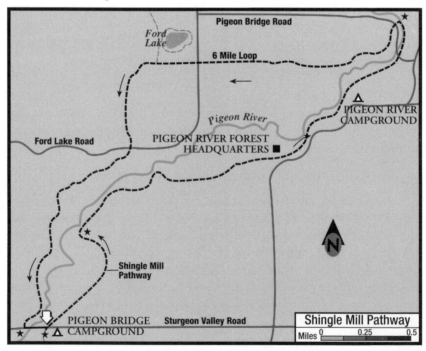

Lake Leelanau Loop

Submitted by Greg and Bobbie Simon

This is a shoreline tour of Lake Michigan, with gently rolling hills and many views of the water, including Grand Traverse Bay and Lake Leelanau. The route passes along beaches and cherry orchards, plus two villages that cater to visitors.

Type of ride: road bike
Starting point: M72 and M22 junction west of Traverse City
Finishing point: same
Distance: 54.9 miles
Level of difficulty: moderate
General terrain: flat to gently rolling along the shorelines of Lake Michigan, Grand Traverse Bay, and Lake Leelanau
Traffic conditions: M22 is a two-lane highway with heavy traffic and a wide shoulder. The rest of the route consists of paved country roads with little traffic.

Leland's Fishtown (photo by: Jim DuFresne)

Estimated riding time: 4 to 7 hours
Best season/time of day to ride: weekdays from late spring to early fall
Points of interest: Lake Michigan, fishing villages, wineries, fruit stands
Accommodations and services: Traverse City offers all services, including grocery stores, restaurants, lodging, and bike shops.
Supplemental maps or other information: none

GETTING THERE

Take the Grandview Parkway in Traverse City to M72, where the parkway ends and M22 begins. The ride can begin anywhere along the parkway, which includes a parallel path for cyclists, hikers, and people on roller blades, up to the intersection with M72.

IN THE SADDLE

Begin at the edge of Traverse City and travel north on M22. You will be cycling in a region well known for its cherry orchards. The French trappers who arrived here in the late 1600s must have recognized the value of the soil and climate, for evidence of cleared lands and apple orchards dating from the seventeenth century were found here two hundred years later. Apples were the first commercial crop, but, in the 1880s, a single acre was planted in cherries. The orchard's yield was abundant, and in the next two decades the forerunners of the present orchards were planted.

After 2 miles of riding, you will come to Cherry Bend and the converted coal docks just past it, which are now the home of the tall ship *Malabar*.

After the ship *Malabar*, M22 becomes a busy country road with an 8-foot paved shoulder to accommodate bike traffic. Ten miles into the ride, the shoulder narrows to 18 inches wide. Grand Traverse Bay is on the right all the way into the village of Suttons Bay at 16 miles. This is a pleasant place to stop for a coffee break or snack.

Continue on M22 to the blinking light and turn left on M204. The road climbs gently for about a mile and then descends for 2 miles to-

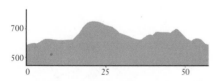

ward the village of Lake Leelanau. Turn right at the bottom of the hill onto County Road 641. After approximately 1/2 mile, there is a Y intersection in the road. Take

The Malabar *sailing on Grand Traverse Bay (photo by: Jim DuFresne)*

the left fork, which is a continuation of 641. This follows the north shoreline of Lake Leelanau.

Six miles later, 641 ends at M22. Turn left and follow M22 south 5 miles into Leland, which includes Fishtown—formerly a fishing wharf and now a small collection of shops. A sawmill was first erected at Leland in 1853. At one time, several sawmills were in operation, and four docks supplied cordwood to the lake steamers that put in for fuel.

Continue south for another 1.5 miles to the intersection with M204. Turn left and travel 3 miles through the village of Lake Leelanau, where you will meet County Road 641 again. Turn right (south) and follow 641 along the shoreline of Lake Leelanau and past a vineyard. County Road 641 ends at Cherry Bend Road, at about 14 miles. Turn left onto Cherry Bend and follow it until it ends at M22. Turn right onto M22 and follow it back to Grandview Parkway.

RIDE GUIDE

★ 0.0 From the city limits of Traverse City, ride north on M22.
   2.0 Cherry Bend.
   16.1 Suttons Bay.
★ 16.3 Turn left onto M204.

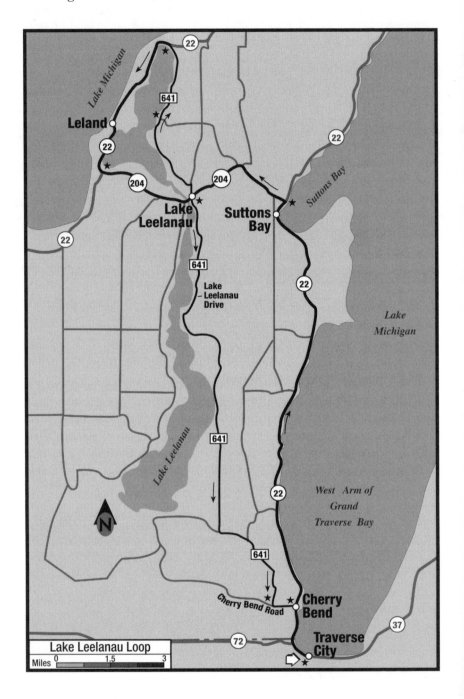

★ 19.4 Turn right onto County Road 641.
★ 19.9 Bear left, following County Road 641.
★ 25.9 Turn left at T intersection onto M22.
   30.9 Leland.
★ 32.4 Turn left onto M204.
★ 35.8 Turn right onto County Road 641.
★ 51.9 Turn left at T intersection onto Cherry Bend Road.
★ 52.9 Cherry Bend. Turn right onto M22.
   54.9 End of ride.

16 Mission Loop
Submitted by Judith Briggs

This ride around the Old Mission Peninsula offers nonstop views of the East and West Arms of Grand Traverse Bay and is a favorite of the Cherry Capital Cycling Club.

Type of ride: road bike
Starting point: Traverse City Central High School parking lot
Finishing point: same
Distance: 38 miles
Level of difficulty: moderate
General terrain: The perimeter road is quite flat; but, wherever the route heads inland, prepare for challenging hills (with great views to reward your efforts).
Traffic conditions: moderate; heavier on some stretches
Estimated riding time: 3 to 5 hours
Best season/time of day to ride: The cherry orchards bloom in mid-May, and July brings warm swimming weather, along with the ripening of the black sweet and red tart cherries. Fall colors usually peak the second week of October. Because of its watery surroundings, the peninsula remains warmer into the fall than much of Michigan and therefore offers good riding relatively late in the year. Avoid riding during morning and afternoon rush hours.
Points of interest: numerous cherry orchards and wineries; quiet

swimming beach and historic lighthouse at about the halfway point, at the tip of the peninsula

Accommodations and services: all services in Traverse City

Supplemental maps or other information: a good map for this ride available for $6.00: Cherry Capital Cycling Club, P.O. Box 1807, Traverse City, MI 49686

GETTING THERE

In Traverse City, turn north off US 31 onto M37. In a half-mile, turn right onto Eastern Avenue and proceed for one long block to the parking lot at Traverse City Central High School.

IN THE SADDLE

From the high school parking lot, ride east to the end of Eastern Avenue and turn left onto Birchwood, which becomes East Shore Road. Following the shoreline, you will notice a mix of quaint old cottages and elegant new homes, the result of recent rapid growth in an area that formerly was just a summer getaway largely filled with cherry orchards. Farther out on the peninsula, the homes become fewer, and orchards still cover much of the land surrounding the small settlement of Old Mission. This is the site of the first white settlement in the Grand Traverse region. In 1839, a Presbyterian mission was established here in a log cabin.

At 1.7 miles, where East Shore Road ends, turn right onto M37/ Center Road, staying far right on the shoulder along this potentially busy road. At the intersection is an access to the East Arm of Grand Traverse Bay, with public toilets. After passing a small vineyard on the right and a large raspberry farm on the left (U-pick in late July), turn right onto Bluff Road at 5.1 miles. You will soon encounter some of the finest views of East Bay to be found.

Follow Bluff Road to its end just past a ninety-degree left-hand curve; at this **T** intersection at 10.0 miles, turn right onto Smokey Hollow Road and prepare for a long gradual climb. At the top, you will ride

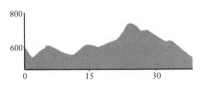

through a tunnel of mature red maples that provide a refreshing shade break after the uphill exertion. The trees are spectacular at their peak colors in mid- to late October.

Old Mission Lighthouse (photo by: Jim DuFresne)

Enjoy the long downhill and follow Smokey Hollow to its end at Mission Road, turning right onto Mission at 13.1 miles and following it through the little settlement. At the **T** intersection at 13.8 miles, turn left onto Swaney Road; then, at 14.7 miles, turn right back onto Center Road/M37. This takes you to the Old Mission Lighthouse, at the northern tip of the peninsula, at 18.0 miles. The point straddles the 45th parallel, midway between the Equator and the North Pole.

The old lighthouse, which guided sailors more than a century ago, is maintained today as a private home. Here you will also find a beautiful shallow-water beach and a picnic area, which provides a good lunch stop if you're carrying lunch. (If you're not, you can ride 5 miles south on Center Road to the corner of Eimen, where you will find a good restaurant—it is a fairly classy one, but well-accustomed to serving cyclists in their strange attire.)

Return south on Center Road/M37, turning right onto Old Mission Road at 22.7 miles. Where the paved road ends at 23.5 miles, turn left onto Peninsula Drive. After 2 miles, and several of the seven hills, turn right at 25.5 miles onto Kroupa Road. Follow this road through several turns (at 26.0 miles, you turn right onto Kroupa Road South);

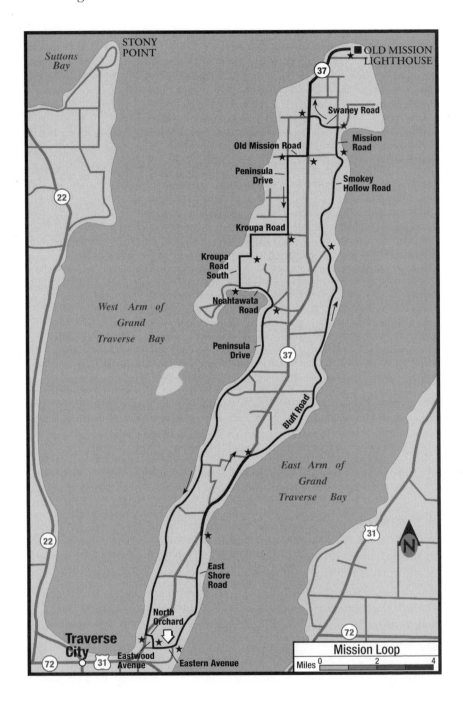

STONY
POINT

*Suttons
Bay*

■ OLD MISSION
LIGHTHOUSE

37

★ Swaney Road

★ Mission
Road

Old Mission Road

Peninsula
Drive

Smokey
Hollow Road

Kroupa Road

Kroupa
Road
South

Neahtawata
Road

*West Arm of
Grand
Traverse Bay*

Peninsula
Drive

37

Bluff Road

*East Arm of
Grand
Traverse Bay*

22

31

N

East
Shore
Road

North
Orchard

**Traverse
City**

72   31

Eastwood
Avenue

Eastern Avenue

72

Mission Loop

Miles 0   2   4

then emerge at Bowers Harbor. Turn left onto Neahtawata Road at mile 27.0 to begin a pleasant cruise along the natural harbor. Just past the parking lot and public access to Bowers Harbor, turn right at the intersection onto Peninsula Drive (mile 28.3) and pass a trio of the Traverse City area's best eateries: the Boat House, the Bowers Harbor Inn, and the Bowery, the most casual of the three.

Peninsula Drive skirts the West Arm of Grand Traverse Bay back into the city, leading through a beautiful neighborhood filled with striking homes and, unfortunately, the heavy traffic that accompanies dense settlement. At the intersection with Center Road at 37.3 miles, make a careful ninety-degree left turn onto North Orchard, following it around onto East Orchard. At 37.5 miles, turn right onto Eastwood Avenue and then left onto Eastern Avenue. Return to the beginning point at 38.0 miles.

RIDE GUIDE

  0.0 From the high school parking lot in Traverse City, ride east on Eastern Avenue.

★ 0.1 Turn left onto Birchwood, which becomes East Shore Road.

★ 1.7 Turn right onto M37.

★ 5.1 Turn right onto Bluff Road.

★ 10.0 Turn right onto Smokey Hollow Road.

★ 13.1 Turn right onto Mission Road.

★ 13.8 At T intersection, turn left onto Swaney Road.

★ 14.7 Turn right onto M37.

★ 18.0 Old Mission Lighthouse and end of M37. Turn around and ride back in the direction from which you came.

★ 22.7 Turn right onto Old Mission Road.

★ 23.5 Turn left onto Peninsula Drive.

★ 25.5 Turn right onto Kroupa Road.

★ 26.0 Turn right onto Kroupa Road South.

★ 27.0 Turn left onto Neahtawata Road.

★ 28.3 Turn right onto Peninsula Drive.

★ 37.3 At the intersection with Center Road, turn left onto North Orchard and follow it around onto East Orchard.

★ 37.5 Turn right onto Eastwood Avenue.

★ 37.6 Turn left onto Eastern Avenue.

  38.0 End of ride.

Cadillac Slide

Submitted by Bruce Baker

This medium-range ride will let you sample the rolling terrain of the Huron-Manistee National Forests, as well as several popular recreation lakes.

Type of ride: road bike
Starting point: Cadillac
Finishing point: same
Distance: 34.5 miles
Level of difficulty: moderate (one climb up Grove Hill)
General terrain: rolling, with some short, steep hills and Grove Hill (at 1,725 feet), the highest point in the Lower Peninsula
Traffic conditions: mostly on lightly traveled two-lane county roads
Estimated riding time: 2 to 4 hours
Best season/time of day to ride: spring through late fall
Points of interest: Grove Hill; Indian burial mounds outside of Cadillac
Accommodations and services: food and water available along route
Supplemental maps or other information: none

GETTING THERE

From Grand Rapids, drive approximately 100 miles north on US 131. In Cadillac, turn onto Lake Street and go to the Cadillac City Hall. Park in the parking lot; 24-hour parking is permitted.

IN THE SADDLE

Cadillac (both the city and the car) were named for Antoine de la Mothe Cadillac, the founder of Detroit. The rolling terrain of the Huron-Manistee National Forests and the proximity of Lake Cadillac and Lake Mitchell have made the town a popular recreational center.

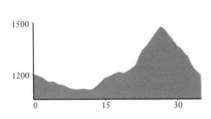

Cadillac was initially settled by timber speculators in 1871, and the village was incorporated in 1877.

As you leave the Cadillac City Hall parking lot, head west on Chestnut Street along Lake Cadillac for 1.2 miles. Turn forty-five degrees to the left onto North Boulevard.

The canal connecting Lakes Cadillac and Mitchell (photo by: Bruce Baker)

At 2.8 miles, take the time to read the history of the Clam Lake logging canal on the historical marker next to the road. Turn left onto M115 between the two lakes. Lake Mitchell will be on your right, and Lake Cadillac on your left. At 3.2 miles, you will pass a pasty shop, where they make a regional dish made popular by the Cornish miners in the 1800s. For the uninitiated, a pasty is a complete meal of meat, potatoes, and vegetables in a pastry crust that the miners took down in the copper and iron mines to eat for lunch.

At 3.3 miles, turn right onto M55 and head southwest. At about 4.5 miles, look to the left through the trees and you will see an Indian burial mound (approximately 5 feet by 12 feet) on the eleventh hole of the Cadillac Country Club golf course. (This may not have been precisely what the Native Americans had in mind, but at least it is preserved.) There are other burial mounds in the area.

At mile 4.6 is the last food and water stop store for the next 11 miles. Turn left onto 33 Road at 5.8 miles. At 9.4 miles, turn left onto County Line Road/Meceloa Road and then right onto 200th Avenue/Diamond

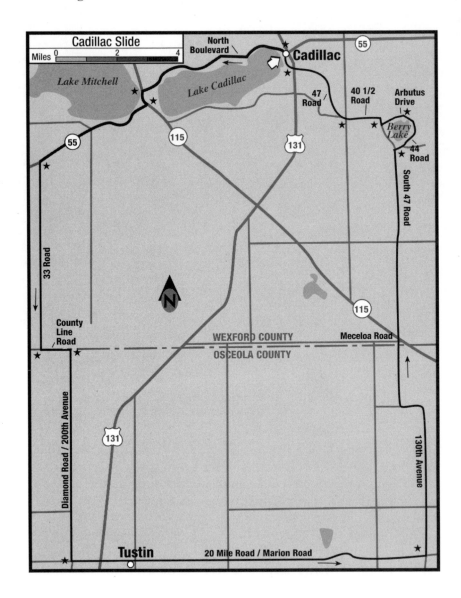

Road. At 14.3 miles, turn left onto 20 Mile Road/Marion Road, crossing the US 131 freeway on your way into Tustin. This is a small Swedish community that is very proud of its heritage. In Tustin, you will cross the unpaved White Pine Rail-Trail, which extends 92 miles between

Cadillac and Grand Rapids. Restaurants and groceries are available in Tustin.

Continue east across the Mackinaw Trail to just over the 20-mile mark in the ride, and turn left onto 130th Avenue. Looking to the north, you can see the highest point in Michigan's Lower Peninsula. This is called Grove Hill, after an early settler. You will reach the summit of Grove Hill (1,725 feet) at mile 23.6.

At just under 26 miles into the ride, you will cross M115 again and ride onto South 47 Road. The South Community Methodist Church will be on your left. At 29.8 miles, turn right onto 44 Road to go around Berry Lake. There is a public fishing landing there with pit toilets but no potable water available. At 29.9 miles, turn left onto Arbutus Drive, and then, in 1 mile, turn right onto an unnamed road. At the junction with 40 ½ Road, bear right. Continue to the junction with 47 Road and bear right again. Follow 47 Road for 2 miles past the US 131 stoplight to Laurel Street. Turn right onto Laurel Street/Lake Street, and you will be back at the parking area.

RIDE GUIDE

★ 0.0 From the Cadillac City Hall parking lot, turn west and ride along Lake Cadillac.
★ 1.2 Turn left onto North Boulevard.
★ 3.0 Turn left onto M115.
★ 3.3 Turn right onto M55.
★ 5.8 Turn left onto 33 Road.
★ 9.4 Turn left onto County Line Road.
★ 9.9 Turn right onto Diamond Road (200th Avenue).
★ 14.3 Turn left onto 20 Mile Road (Marion Road).
★ 20.2 Turn left onto 130th Avenue.
   23.6 Grove Hill.
   25.9 Cross M115 and ride onto South 47 Road.
★ 29.8 Turn right onto 44 Road.
★ 29.9 Bear left onto Arbutus Drive.
★ 30.9 Turn right onto an unnamed road.
★ 31.1 Turn left onto 40 ½ Road.
★ 32.8 Turn right onto 47 Road.
★ 34.0 Turn right onto Laurel Street (Lake Street).
★ 34.5 Cadillac City Hall parking lot. End of ride.

Bellaire Century

18

Submitted by Don Parry

This challenging, almost-a-century ride passes through several small towns, and proffers scenic vistas of immense Lake Michigan and its Little Traverse Bay, as well as "small" lakes, such as Charlevoix and Walloon.

Type of ride: road bike
Starting point: the public parking lot in Bellaire
Finishing point: Fort Michilimackinac State Park near Mackinaw City
Distance: 95.7 miles
Level of difficulty: difficult
General terrain: hilly
Traffic conditions: generally light
Estimated riding time: 7 to 10 hours
Best season/time of day to ride: best in fall; quieter on weekdays
Points of interest: an abundance of scenic highlights, including the "tunnel of trees" along Beach Road outside Petoskey and a parade of fabulous homes fronting Little Traverse Bay in the Harbor Springs area; the world-famous Mackinac (pronounced mack-i-naw) Bridge, or "Mighty Mac," that connects the Lower and Upper Peninsulas over the 5-mile-wide Straits of Mackinac
Accommodations and services: all services available along the way
Supplemental maps or other information: maps for Charlevoix, Antrim, and Emmet Counties available from the Michigan Department of Transportation

GETTING THERE
From I-75 North, take exit 270 (Waters). Go north to Mancelona Road (C38); then west to Mancelona. From there, take M88 northwest to Bellaire.

IN THE SADDLE
The route begins in Bellaire, population 1,004, which is situated in an area rich in cycling and other recreational opportunities; it then heads north through Antrim County, where mornings often are foggy and the countryside teems with deer and wild turkey. The route can be ridden in two days, with an overnight at the halfway point in Petoskey, or it

can be accomplished as a tough one-day ride. It ends near Mackinaw City—the only place, it is said, where one can watch the sun rise over one of the Great Lakes (Huron) and set over another (Michigan).

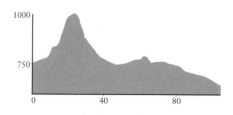

From the Bellaire parking lot, ride east on the Bellaire Highway. At 1.9 miles, turn left onto Derenzy Road. Turn right onto Old State Road at mile 6.4; then, at 8.5 miles, turn left onto Kramer Road. Turn right onto Murphy Road at 9.4 miles and left onto Kidder Road at mile 9.8. At 13.6 miles, turn right onto Rogers Road, and, at 14.5 miles, turn left onto M32, bearing left at 15.9 to continue following that road. At 16.3, in East Jordan, the first large town encountered, turn right onto Main Street. Then, at 16.5, go left onto Division Street and immediately right onto Boyne Road. At 16.9 miles, turn right onto Peninsula Road; then, at mile 17.2, turn left onto Advance Road.

Four miles down the road, at mile 21.2, turn right onto Lake Shore Drive and continue along the shore of Lake Charlevoix. At 23.1 miles,

The route skirts around Walloon Lake. (photo by: Don Parry)

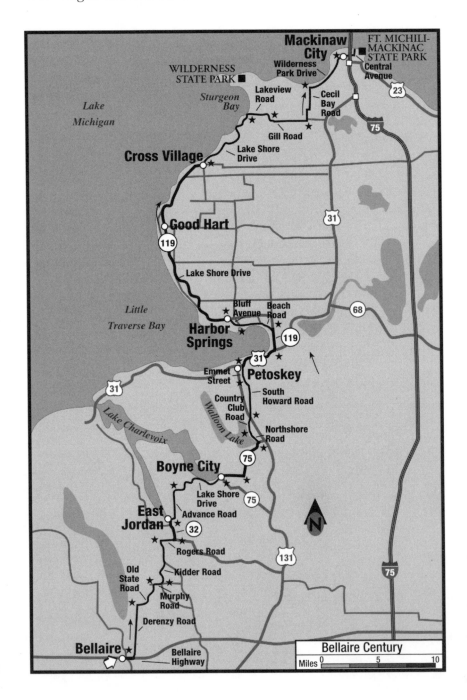

Mackinaw City

FT. MICHILI-
MACKINAC
STATE PARK

WILDERNESS
STATE PARK

Wilderness
Park Drive

Central
Avenue

23

Lakeview
Road

*Sturgeon
Bay*

Cecil Bay
Road

*Lake
Michigan*

Gill Road

75

Cross Village

Lake Shore
Drive

31

Good Hart

119

Lake Shore Drive

68

*Little
Traverse Bay*

Bluff
Avenue

Beach
Road

**Harbor
Springs**

119

31

Emmet
Street

Petoskey

31

South
Howard Road

Country
Club
Road

Walloon Lake

Northshore
Road

Lake Charlevoix

75

Boyne City

Lake Shore
Drive

75

**East
Jordan**

Advance Road

32

Rogers Road

131

Kidder Road

Old
State
Road

N

75

Murphy
Road

Derenzy Road

Bellaire

Bellaire
Highway

Bellaire Century

Miles 0   5   10

go left onto Division Street and then, at 23.3 miles, turn left onto Front Street. In Boyne City, turn right at mile 24.3 onto Court Street. At 25.2 miles, ride onto North Wildwood Harbor Road; turn right 3.1 miles later onto Shadow Trail, at mile 28.3. At 30.4 miles, turn left onto South Shore Drive; then, at mile 31.5, turn left onto M75. Turn left onto West Street at 32.4 miles and left onto Northshore Road at 32.6 miles.

At 34.1 miles, turn right onto Country Club Road, proceeding left onto South Howard Road at mile 35.6. Four miles beyond, at mile 39.6, ride onto Standish Avenue at the railroad tracks. Enter Petoskey, a bustling burg perched on Lake Michigan's Little Traverse Bay. The town's name is an English approximation of the name of the Indian chief who owned most of the surrounding lands when the first European settlers arrived.

Bear left at 40.3 miles onto Emmet Street. Turn right onto US 31 at mile 42.3 and continue 2.2 miles to M119, where you turn left. Turn left onto Beach Road at 46.9 miles and ride through the striking "tunnel of trees." At 48.9 miles, go right onto Bluff Avenue. Turn left onto M119 again at mile 49.1 and ride through Harbor Springs; then turn right onto Hoyt Street at 50.6 miles. At mile 50.8, go left onto Lake Road and, after 2 miles, go right onto M119 (Lake Shore Drive) at mile 52.8. Continue along M119 for almost 20 miles, passing through the towns of Good Hart and Cross Village, where a stop at Leg's Inn is recommended. Beyond Cross Village, the terrain flattens out a bit.

Bear left at 72.3 miles onto Lake Shore Drive and continue for 6.5 miles. At 78.8 miles, turn right onto Lakeview Road; then left onto Gill Road after 3 miles, at mile 81.8. Turn left onto Cecil Bay Road at mile 85.1. At mile 88.4, turn right onto Wilderness Park Drive, from which you will earn your first views of the distant spires of the Mackinac Bridge. Turn right onto Trails End Road at mile 92.0 and left onto Nohomis Street at 93.3 miles. At mile 94.3, go right onto West Central Avenue; then left onto Central Avenue at 95.2 miles. Reach your destination of Fort Michilimackinac State Park at 95.7 miles.

RIDE GUIDE

★   0.0 From Bellaire parking lot, ride east on Bellaire Highway.
★   1.9 Turn left onto Derenzy Road.
★   6.4 Turn right onto Old State Road.
★   8.5 Turn left onto Kramer Road.

★   9.4 Turn right onto Murphy Road.
★   9.8 Turn left onto Kidder Road.
★ 13.6 Turn right onto Rogers Road.
★ 14.5 Turn left onto M32.
      15.9 Bear left to continue on M32.
★ 16.3 East Jordan.Turn right onto Main Street.
★ 16.5 Turn left onto Division Street and then immediately right
        onto Boyne Road.
★ 16.9 Turn right onto Peninsula Road.
★ 17.2 Turn left onto Advance Road.
★ 21.2 Turn right onto Lake Shore Drive.
★ 23.1 Turn left onto Division Street.
★ 23.3 Turn left onto Front Street.
★ 24.3 Boyne City. Right onto Court Street.
      25.2 Ride onto North Wildwood Harbor Road.
★ 28.3 Turn right onto Shadow Trail.
★ 30.4 Turn left onto South Shore Drive.
★ 31.5 Turn left onto M75.
★ 32.4 Turn left onto West Street.
★ 32.6 Turn left onto Northshore Road.
★ 34.1 Turn right onto Country Club Road.
★ 35.6 Turn left onto South Howard Road.
      39.6 At the railroad tracks, ride onto Standish Avenue.
★ 40.3 Petoskey. Bear left onto Emmet Street.
★ 42.3 Turn right onto US 31.
★ 44.5 Turn left onto M119.
★ 46.9 Turn left onto Beach Road.
★ 48.9 Turn right onto Bluff Avenue.
★ 49.1 Turn left onto M119. Harbor Springs.
★ 50.6 Turn right onto Hoyt Street.
★ 50.8 Turn left onto Lake Road.
★ 52.8 Turn right onto M119 (Lake Shore Drive).
★ 72.3 Bear left to continue on Lake Shore Drive. M119 leaves
        route.
★ 78.8 Turn right onto Lakeview Road.
★ 81.8 Turn left onto Gill Road.
★ 85.1 Turn left onto Cecil Bay Road.
★ 88.4 Turn right onto Wilderness Park Drive.

A unique rest stop—Legs Inn in Cross Village (photo by: Don Parry)

- ★ 92.0 Turn right onto Trails End Road.
- ★ 93.3 Turn left onto Nohomis Street.
- ★ 94.3 Turn right onto West Central Avenue.
- ★ 95.2 Turn left onto Central Avenue.
- ★ 95.7 Ft. Michilimackinac State Park. End of ride.

19 Harbor Springs Tour
Submitted by Terry Kureth

Climb from the shores of Lake Michigan to the high bluffs south of Cross Village, passing through deciduous and evergreen forests.

Type of ride: road bike
Starting point: Harbor Springs City Park
Finishing point: same
Distance: 20.2 miles
Level of difficulty: easy to moderate

General terrain: initial steep hill leads to flat terrain with some roll-
  ing hills
Traffic conditions: heavier resort traffic on weekends on M119
Estimated riding time: 2 hours
Best season/time of day to ride: late spring and fall, during the week
  to avoid resort area traffic
Points of interest: fall colors, views of Lake Michigan
Accommodations and services: grocery stores, restaurants, hotels, and
  parking near starting point
Supplemental maps or other information: none

GETTING THERE
From Traverse City, travel for 70 miles on US 31 to the junction with
M119. Turn left onto M119 and travel 7 miles to Harbor Springs City
Park on Main Street/M119, near the Pier Restaurant.

IN THE SADDLE
Ride north up a short steep incline through a residential area to the top
of bluffs overlooking Lake Michigan. A half mile into the ride is the first
sign for Cross Village, 20 miles away. At 3.4 miles is the Thorne Swift
Nature Preserve, a thirty-acre parcel donated to West Traverse Township that includes a nature center and observation platform.

  After a series of hills at 4 miles, the route breaks into open country.
At the intersection of M119 and Terpening Road, the road turns left

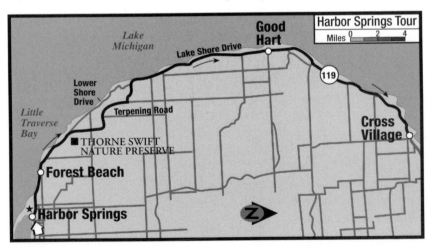

and then back to the right. Here, the route enters another forested area before entering the village of Good Hart at the 13-mile mark. Good Hart includes a grocery store and picnic areas. From Good Hart, the route is level the rest of the way to Cross Village.

From Cross Village, if you wish you may simply retrace your path back to Harbor Springs on M119. Another option, with different scenery, is to return to Harbor Springs by riding about 100 yards south from Leg's Inn on M119 and turning left on State Road. This road includes more farm country and fewer trees than M119 and can be a sweaty 20 miles in the sun on a hot day. The last option is to continue north and east for another 20 miles to Mackinaw City, the Straits of Mackinac, and the "Big Mac" bridge between Michigan's Upper and Lower Peninsulas.

RIDE GUIDE

★   0.0 From the public parking lot in Harbor Springs, ride north for one block and then turn left onto M119 (Lake Shore Drive).

2.1 Forest Beach.

3.4 Thorne Swift Nature Preserve.

13.1 Good Hart.

20.2 Cross Village. End of ride.

Manistee Forest Ride
Submitted by Bruce Baker

The majority of this ride is within the Huron-Manistee National Forests. Watch for wildlife—you might even see a black bear, although they are known for their inherent bashfulness.

Type of ride: road bike
Starting point: Cadillac
Finishing point: same
Distance: 98 miles
Level of difficulty: moderate
General terrain: gently rolling

Traffic conditions: lightly traveled, all paved county and state roads
Estimated riding time: 6 to 10 hours
Best season/time of day to ride: spring through fall
Points of interest: a lot of lakes and wildlife
Accommodations and services: small stores and restaurants along the
    route
Supplemental maps or other information: none

GETTING THERE
From Grand Rapids, drive approximately 100 miles north on US 131.
In Cadillac, turn onto Lake Street and go to the Cadillac City Hall. Park
in the parking lot; 24-hour parking is permitted.

IN THE SADDLE
Cadillac was initially settled by timber speculators in 1871, and the
village was incorporated in 1877. Both the city and the car were named
for Antoine de la Mothe Cadillac, the founder of Detroit. The rolling terrain of the Huron-Manistee National Forests and the proximity of Lakes Cadillac and Mitchell have made the town a popular
recreational center.

As you leave the Cadillac City Hall parking lot on Chestnut, head
west along Lake Cadillac. At just under 1 mile, next to a football field,
turn right onto Linden. Follow Linden for 0.3 mile and turn left onto
West Division Street. Continue onto Division Street.

Continue across M115 to East Lake Mitchell Drive and turn right
at the stop sign after crossing the railroad tracks. Then turn left and go
for 0.4 mile to 33½ Road. Turn right onto 33½ Road. At the 6-mile
point, turn left onto 34 Road.

At 11.2 miles, cross another set of railroad tracks. Use caution! This
uneven set of rails can upset a bike if you are not careful.

At mile 11.5, turn right onto No. 23 Road toward Boon. At 13.6,
ride straight onto No. 30 Road, which continues to run parallel to the

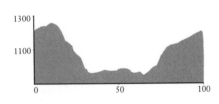

railroad tracks. There is a nice
gradual downhill section for about
6 miles into Harrietta. At mile
18.4 turn left onto Michigan Avenue, then immediately turn right
onto Schlagle/No. 30 Road.

Caution: There is another bad set of railroad tracks to cross at just over 19 miles. Shortly after this crossing, you will pass the Harrietta Fish Hatchery; drop in for a visit if you have the time. There are restrooms available here.

At 21.7 miles, cross M37 (food available here) and pass a small airstrip (Bunch Field) on your left. Two miles past the strip, follow No. 30 Road around a corner to the south and continue to the junction with Coates Highway at mile 26.5. Follow Coates Highway and look forward to the fast downhill run you will have to the crossing of the Manistee River at just over 28 miles into your ride.

The Manistee River was one of the four most important "log highways" during the lumber boom in northern Michigan (the other three rivers were the Saginaw, the Muskegon, and the Menominee). The town of Manistee was built at the mouth of the Manistee River and became a primary lumbering town.

There are several food stops available in the town of Brethren, which was the boyhood home of well-known actor James Earl Jones. At the Brethren Village Park (on your left at 36.1 miles) there are restrooms and water available. Turn left at the park onto North High Bridge Road and again cross the Manistee River.

At the junction with M55, at mile 41.7, turn left onto M55 (also called the Caberfae Highway). Travel for 1.4 miles on M55 and then

A park beside Lake Cadillac (photo by: Bruce Baker)

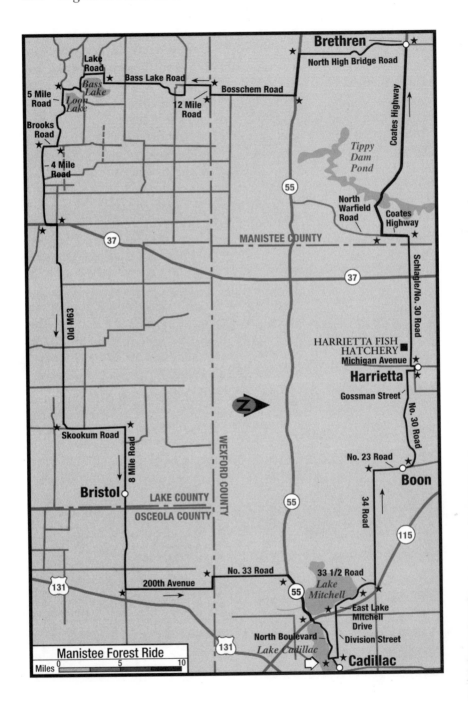

Manistee Forest Ride

Miles 0   5   10

turn south (right) onto Bosschem Road/County Road 669. After a little more than 4 miles, at mile 47.9, turn right by an abandoned gravel pit onto 12 Mile Road. Follow the county line (Manistee County/Lake County) for 0.5 mile; then turn south (left) on Bass Lake Road. This road takes you through two groupings of numerous small lakes, including (surprise!) Bass Lake. There are food stops available at 50.5 and 56.3 miles. At the south end of Bass Lake, turn right to follow the west shore of Loon Lake. At the 60-mile point in the ride, if you look closely you will see that you are riding along an old abandoned logging railroad grade. Turn left onto 5 Mile Road and cross the south end of Loon Lake. Brooks Road and 4 Mile Road will take you to the junction with M37. Turn left onto M37 and, in less than a mile, turn right onto 5 Mile Road/Old M63. There is a restaurant at 68.6 miles.

Caution: At 71.3 miles, continue straight east rather than following the right-hand curve as you might expect. At the junction with Skookum Road, turn north (left) onto Skookum Road. Three miles later, turn right onto 8 Mile Road. There is a food stop in Bristol at 81.2 miles. At 86.1 miles, turn left onto 200th Avenue/Diamond Road. After a quick jog to the left on County Line/Meceloa Road, 200th Avenue becomes No. 33 Road.

At 94.6 miles, turn right onto M55. Get in the left turn lane at the stoplight at M115 and go 0.3 miles before turning right onto North Boulevard by the canal. Follow North Boulevard back into Cadillac; follow Chestnut back to the city hall parking lot.

RIDE GUIDE

- ★ 0.0 From the Cadillac City Hall parking lot, ride west along Lake Cadillac.
- ★ 0.7 Turn right onto Linden.
- ★ 1.0 Turn left onto West Division Street.
- ★ 2.0 Ride onto Division Street.
- ★ 3.1 Turn right onto East Lake Mitchell Drive.
- ★ 3.5 Turn right onto 33½ Road.
- ★ 6.0 Turn left onto 34 Road.
- ★ 11.5 Turn right onto No. 23 Road.
- ★ 13.6 Ride straight onto No. 30 Road.
  16.7 Cross No. 15½ Road and ride onto Gossman Street.
- ★ 18.0 Turn right onto Caberfae Road.

The Clam Lake Canal (photo by: Bruce Baker)

★ 18.3 Turn left onto Gaston Avenue.
★ 18.4 Turn left onto Michigan Avenue, and then turn right onto Schlagle (No. 30 Road).
    19.2 Harrietta Fish Hatchery.
★ 21.7 Cross M37 and follow road to Coates Highway.
★ 26.5 Follow Coates Highway to the right.
★ 35.4 Turn left onto North High Bridge Road.

★ 41.7 Turn left onto M55.
★ 43.1 Turn right onto Bosschem Road.
★ 47.9 Turn right onto 12 Mile Road (Peters Farm Road).
★ 48.4 Turn left onto Bass Lake Road.
★ 56.3 Turn right onto Lake Road.
★ 57.2 Turn left onto 5 Mile Road.
★ 59.8 Turn right onto Brooks Road.
★ 60.4 Turn left onto 4 Mile Road.
★ 64.8 Turn left onto M37.
★ 65.3 Turn right onto Old M63.
  71.3 Ride straight to continue on Old M63.
★ 76.3 Bear left onto Skookum Road.
★ 79.3 Turn right onto 8 Mile Road.
★ 86.1 Turn left onto 200th Avenue.
★ 90.6 After a jog left onto County Line Road, route becomes No. 33 Road.
★ 94.6 Turn right onto M55.
★ 94.9 Turn right onto North Boulevard.
★ 96.7 Turn right onto Chestnut Street.
★ 98.0 Cadillac City Hall. End of ride.

21 Harbor Springs Loop

Submitted by Kerry Irons

This ride is located along Lake Michigan's eastern shore near Little Traverse Bay. It includes a lot of hills, big and small, as well as plenty of opportunities to stop and visit in small towns and villages along the way.

Type of ride: road bike
Starting point: downtown Harbor Springs
Finishing point: same
Distance: 54 miles
Level of difficulty: moderate
General terrain: flat terrain, with some rolling hills
Traffic conditions: two-lane roads with very light traffic except near Harbor Springs

Estimated riding time: 3.5 to 4.5 hours
Best season/time of day to ride: late spring and fall, during the week
   to avoid resort area traffic
Points of interest: Harbor Springs resort community with marina and
   Victorian houses; designated scenic highway (M119) between Cross
   Village and Harbor Springs
Accommodations and services: all services available in Harbor Springs
Supplemental maps or other information: none

GETTING THERE
From I-75, take M32 west to US 131 North. Connect with M119 to
downtown Harbor Springs. Parking is available in the harbor lot.

IN THE SADDLE
The ride begins in Harbor Springs, a summer resort community
built by Chicago's elite in the early part of this century that has many
Victorian houses, several golf courses, and a marina. Ride east from
the marina parking lot and head uphill for 4 miles to Pleasant View
Road. Turn left, and the route climbs toward two ski areas.

At the 13-mile mark, the road jogs to the right for 0.5 mile at
Robinson Road and then turns north again on Pleasant View Road.
There are several climbs on this portion of the route, but they are
rewarded by good views of the lake country. Continue straight at the
stop sign on Levering Road at mile 20 into the small town of Bliss.

Just past Bliss, on the Sturgeon Bay Trail, there is an abrupt climb
to a hilltop with a view of Lake Michigan, followed by a gentle 4-mile
decline and a left turn onto Lake Shore Drive at mile 28. Follow this
road for 18 miles to the last significant hill of the ride. The route passes
through small rolling hills formed by sand dunes above Lake Michigan
and enters Cross Village, named for a cross placed on a nearby bluff by
early settlers.

After leaving Cross Village, Lake Shore Drive becomes M119,
which leads all the way back to Harbor Springs. Along the way, you will

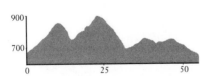

pass several bluffs above Lake Michigan and the town of Good Hart at
mile 40. At mile 46, the road leaves
the lake shore and heads into the
toughest climb of the ride, which

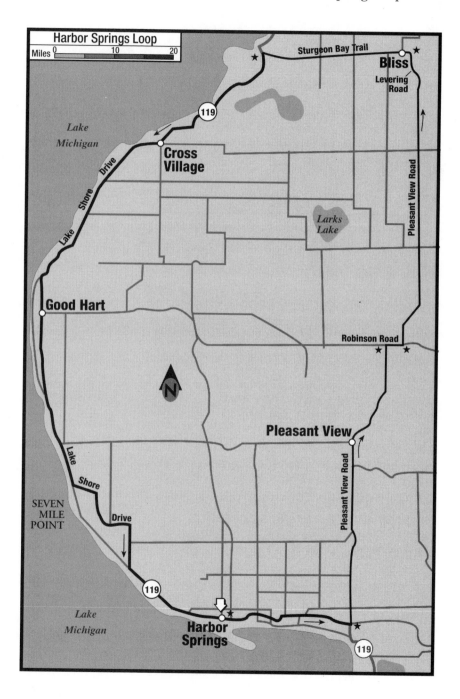

Harbor Springs Loop

Miles 0   10   20

Lake
Michigan

119

Cross
Village

Lake Shore Drive

Good Hart

SEVEN
MILE
POINT

Lake
Shore

Drive

119

Lake
Michigan

Harbor
Springs

Sturgeon Bay Trail

Bliss

Levering
Road

Pleasant View Road

Larks
Lake

Robinson Road

Pleasant View

Pleasant View Road

N

119

The Harbor Springs Marina (photo by: Kerry Irons)

extends for about a mile. From the top of the hill, the last 7 miles are all downhill into Harbor Springs.

RIDE GUIDE
- ★   0.0 From the Harbor Springs Marina parking lot, turn right onto M119.
- ★   4.0 Turn left onto Pleasant View Road.
- ★ 13.2 Turn right onto Robinson Road.
- ★ 13.7 Turn left onto Pleasant View Road.
-    20.1 Ride straight onto Levering Road.
- ★ 23.3 The route changes to Sturgeon Bay Trail.
-    23.5 Bliss and store.
- ★ 27.9 Turn left onto Lake Shore Drive (M119).
-    32.7 Cross Village.
-    40.0 Good Hart.
-    53.8 Go straight to continue on Lake Shore Drive (M119).
-    54.0 Marina parking lot. End of ride.

Green Lake Loop

Submitted by Carol Otto

This ride is a loop around a lake situated at the base of the Leelanau Peninsula, south of Traverse City. This area is an important part of Michigan's fruit district; you will see many cherry and peach orchards.

Type of ride: road bike
Starting point: Karlin
Finishing point: same
Distance: 12.5 miles
Level of difficulty: easy
General terrain: flat
Traffic conditions: light on county roads; heavier near Interlochen and Interlochen State Park
Estimated riding time: 1 to 2 hours
Best season/time of day to ride: spring through fall
Points of interest: scenic views of lakes; Interlochen Center for the Arts
Accommodations and services: food available in Interlochen
Supplemental maps or other information: for concerts and festival schedules at Interlochen: Interlochen Center for the Arts, P.O. Box 199, Interlochen, MI 49643, (616) 276-7200

GETTING THERE

From Traverse City, drive south on US 31 for 15 miles. At the junction with M137, turn left (south) onto County Road 137. Drive through Interlochen and continue south on County Road 137 to the town of Karlin. You can also start this loop ride at Interlochen State Park, where additional parking is available.

IN THE SADDLE

Several of the small towns in the vicinity of Green Lake, such as Grawn and Karlin, began as lumbering communities but are now supported through orchards and the recreation industries.

From Karlin, ride north on Karlin Road/County Road 137 toward Green Lake. You will pass the Green Lake landing strip and travel over a narrow spit of land between Green Lake (to the west) and Duck Lake (to the east). You will ride past 187-acre Interlochen State Park, which offers restrooms, water, and a great site for a picnic.

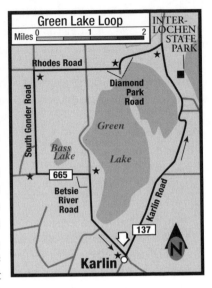

At the 5-mile point, turn left onto Diamond Park Road. Just to the north is the headquarters of the famous summer school for music and the arts. Founded in 1928, Interlochen began as a national high school orchestra and band camp. Initially a 400-acre site, today the campus occupies 1,200 acres. In the 1930s, the camp was divided into boys' and girls' facilities, with the young men at Lake Wahbekaness, and the young women at Lake Wahbekanetta. (Sounds like a plot line for a Bill Murray movie.) In later years, the camp expanded into other areas and is now called the Interlochen Center for the Arts. Students are enrolled for eight weeks each summer in music, art, drama, or dance. Visitors are welcome to tour the grounds. Check at the center for open concerts or rehearsals.

At 6.6 miles, turn right to continue on Diamond Park Road, which merges into Rhodes Road. At the intersection of Rhodes Road and South Gonder Road, turn left (south) onto South Gonder Road. At just under 8 miles, turn left onto Betsie River Road (County Road 665). Follow this road around the south end of Bass Lake and then Green Lake, back to the intersection with Karlin Road/County Road 137. Turn right onto Karlin Road at 12.4 miles and ride back into Karlin.

RIDE GUIDE

    0.0 From Karlin, ride north on County Road 137 (Karlin Road).
★   5.1 Turn left onto Diamond Park Road.
★   6.6 Turn right to continue on Diamond Park Road.
    7.2 Ride straight onto Rhodes Road.
★   7.8 Turn left onto South Gonder Road.
★   8.8 Turn left onto County Road 665 (Betsie River Road).
★   10.8 Turn right to continue on County Road 665 (Betsie River Road).
★   12.4 Turn right onto County Road 137 (Karlin Road).
    12.5 Karlin. End of ride.

Region 3:
Southwest Michigan

The world's largest weather vane (photo by: Vern Cascaddan)

Grand Haven Trail

23

Submitted by Michael Vanderveen

This mid-range ride takes you along the Lake Michigan shore between Grand Haven and Holland. It is an easy ride and quite suitable for a family that has some cycling experience.

Type of ride: road bike
Starting point: Grand Haven State Park
Finishing point: Holland
Distance: 21.1 miles
Level of difficulty: easy
General terrain: flat
Traffic conditions: choice of either a separate bike path or a two-lane road with medium traffic
Estimated riding time: 2 hours
Best season/time of day to ride: spring through fall
Points of interest: heavily wooded area with scenic views of Lake Michigan
Accommodations and services: all services available along the bike path or in the towns at either end of the ride
Supplemental maps or other information: none

GETTING THERE

From Grand Rapids, follow I-96 west for 28 miles to Grand Haven.

IN THE SADDLE

Grand Haven is situated at the mouth of the Grand River, which gives the city an excellent harbor. The 7-mile-long Spring Lake connects Grand Haven and Lake Michigan. The city has long been based around its shipping and commercial fishing activities.

Your ride begins at Grand Haven State Park. Before beginning your ride, take a stroll on the boardwalk and out onto the pier to the lighthouse.

Leaving the park, head south along the beach, making a left turn onto Grand Avenue. At 1.5 miles, turn right onto Sheldon Road at the intersection of Sheldon Road and Robbins Road. The bike path begins on the east side of Sheldon Road.

The beach is a welcome sight at the end of a long day. (photo by: Michael Vanderveen)

Proceed south through the city's residential area. At 3.1 miles, you will pass Rosy Mound on your right. This is a sand dune that rises from the edge of the roadway—a well-known landmark among locals.

Continue riding south through beautiful hardwood beech forests. When you reach the 7-mile point, you will see the Lake Michigan filtration plant, which supplies water from the lake to some half a million people in western Michigan.

Traverse the boardwalk and note the wetlands, Pigeon River, and the lake. On weekends, the public boat launch is crowded (maybe overcrowded). Access to Lake Michigan and its perch, salmon, and steelhead fishing is a big attraction.

Continue past Camp Blodgett. At 8.8 miles, you will pass Kirk Park. In season, this is a good rest-and-relaxation stop, with food, water, beach, and shade. It is worth a stop just for the view of the beautiful beaches.

Pass Port Sheldon at 12 miles and turn right onto Lake Shore Avenue at 12.3 miles (Sandy Point Restaurant will be on your right). The trail's terrain becomes more rolling after this point. There is a water and rest area at Port Sheldon Township Park, located at 14.7 miles.

At 16 miles, there is a gazebo on the left side of the trail that has water available. At 19.8 miles, you will arrive at Tunnel Park, which has food and water in season. Climb the dunes to view Lake Michigan or take the easier route through the tunnel.

At 21 miles, your route intersects Ottawa Beach Road. Turn right (west) to reach Holland State Park. There is food and camping available here. Turn left (east) to reach the city of Holland, which is approximately 5 miles farther along Ottawa Beach Road. Holland has all services.

As you may have guessed, a large percentage of Holland's population is of Dutch descent. The circumstances surrounding the arrival of the Dutch in Michigan are similar to the circumstances that drove the Puritans to New England. In the mid-1840s, secessionists of the Dutch State Church were feeling persecuted by civil authorities. In the fall of 1846, Dr. A. C. Van Raalte, a secessionist pastor, sailed from Holland

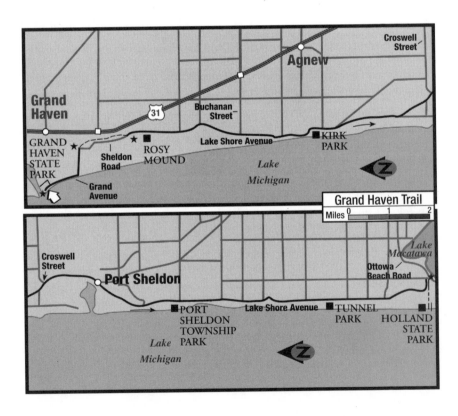

A nice, smooth trail to begin the ride (photo by: Michael Vanderveen)

with fifty-three followers. They purchased 1,000 acres of government land in early 1847 and founded the city of Holland, Michigan.

They platted their city at the mouth of the Black River on Lake Macatawa, a thin finger of Lake Michigan that reaches 6 miles inland. In May, the annual Tulip Time festival is held here, which attracts many thousands of visitors.

RIDE GUIDE
- ★   0.0 From Grand Haven State Park, ride south on Grand Avenue.
- ★   1.5 Turn right onto Sheldon Road and ride onto the bike path on the east side of Sheldon Road.
- ★   2.6 Ride onto Lake Shore Avenue.
     3.1 Rosy Mound.
    12.3 Bear right to continue on Lake Shore Avenue.
    14.7 Port Sheldon Township Park.
    19.8 Tunnel Park.
- ★ 21.1 Holland State Park. End of ride.

Last Train to Clarksville
24
Submitted by John Prius

Follow old railroad trunk lines from the town of Ada through the town of Lowell and the quiet farm community in the surrounding area.

Type of ride: road bike
Starting point: Ada Park in the town of Ada
Finishing point: same
Distance: 41.5 miles
Level of difficulty: easy to moderate
General terrain: rolling hills to level
Traffic conditions: mostly light traffic on two-lane roads
Estimated riding time: 4 hours
Best season/time of day to ride: May through October; an especially good fall-color ride
Points of interest: nice vistas
Accommodations and services: Village Bike Shop between Cascade and Ada on Thornapple Drive; food available in Ada, Clarksville, and Lowell
Supplemental maps or other information: Kent County road map available at the Ada Township Hall or at local service stations

GETTING THERE
From Highway M21 in Grand Rapids, take the Flint exit and travel east on East Fulton Street for about 5 miles to the town of Ada. Turn right on Ada Drive and go to Thornapple River Drive. Turn left and proceed to the covered bridge, which has parking on the left.

IN THE SADDLE
Located where the Thornapple River joins the Grand River, the town of Ada was founded in 1821. A historical marker on the main street (M21) notes the site of the Rix Robinson Trading Post, named for the region's first white settler and the post's proprietor. Once the home of lumber mills, today Ada is better known as the home of the Amway Corporation.

Begin your ride on Fase Street, across from the parking lot near the covered bridge. At Buttrick Avenue, turn right and cross the railroad

The Ada covered bridge (photo by: John Prius)

tracks. Immediately proceed onto the bike path to the left, which will take you to Centennial Park. Restrooms are available here, along with additional parking should the lot at the covered bridge be full. There is also a nature trail, as well as several nice areas for picnicking.

Continue south on Buttrick Avenue to a short, steep climb that will awaken your muscles and get your blood moving. The route here is over rolling hills and past large old homesteads, interspersed with newer luxury homes. (The older homesteads look best, don't you think?)

At 4.7 miles, use caution while riding down a steep hill; there is a stop sign immediately at the base of the hill, so you do not want to build up too much speed. Proceed straight ahead to Whitneyville Road, where you will turn left and ride to the railroad crossing. Do not cross the tracks; turn left onto 52nd Street and travel east over more rolling hills. You will pass farms and rows of trees (wind breaks) where you might see deer. The fields here are filled with wildflowers in the spring months.

At Alden Nash Road, 11 miles into your ride, there is a stone fence with a lot of shade, which provides a great spot for a short break. There is a strange-looking homestead here that serves well as a conversation piece.

Continue east on 52nd Street. Your route is flat now for about 9 miles. At the intersection of 52nd Street and Pratt Lake Avenue, where you will see a "Boot and Scoot" sign, turn right onto Pratt Lake Avenue. At 14.7 miles, turn left onto 64th Street and ride into Ionia County. Follow a long S-curve and then enter Clarksville. Is this the Clarksville immortalized in the song by The Monkees? Who knows. In any event, your route does follow two different railroad trunk lines.

Turn right onto Bell Road and then left onto Clarksville Road. Clarksville boasts a hardware store, several cafes, a filling station, and not much else. In any event, you are at the 20-mile point in your ride, and the town makes a nice rest and lunch stop. Then it is time to make your way back towards Ada.

Turn left (north) at the blinker light that you passed as you came into Clarksville; this puts you onto Nash Highway. Follow the highway for 3 miles to the intersection with Grand River Avenue. Turn left onto Grand River Avenue and ride past the "Kids, Kows, and Konfusion" sign to Hastings Road. Turn right onto Hastings Road (watch for Jimmy's Grill at the corner) and continue over more rolling hills and through pastures of wildflowers. The road will make a few curves and change its name: Keep following the yellow centerline. Watch for a huge wire sculpture of a fly on your right.

At mile 29, begin a mile-long descent into the town of Lowell. Turn right onto Grand River Avenue, which becomes Division Street as you

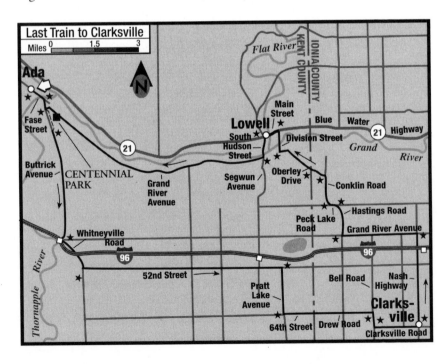

cross the Grand River. Lowell was settled in 1821 at the juncture of the Flat River and the Grand River. Prior to the settlers' arrival, there was a permanent Indian village here with approximately four hundred residents.

At Main Street, turn left and ride through Lowell. Then cross the Grand River again. You will see the Lowell Showboat, which occasionally hosts concerts. At South Hudson Street, where you will find one of the few traffic lights on this route, turn left and pedal past the Big King Milling Company and the 4-H Fairgrounds, on your left, where you might catch a horse show in progress.

Cross the Grand River once more and turn right onto Grand River Avenue. This is the final stretch of road back to Centennial Park. Ahead is 9 miles of flat, shady riding—a great end to a beautiful ride. At Buttrick Avenue, turn right. Then turn left onto Fase Street, which leads to the bike path. Return to the covered bridge in Ada.

RIDE GUIDE

★   0.0 From the parking lot by the covered bridge in Ada, ride south on Fase Street.

★   0.3 Turn right onto Buttrick Avenue and immediately bear left onto the bike path that runs parallel to Buttrick Avenue.

　 0.7 Centennial Park. Ride onto Buttrick Avenue and continue south.

★   4.7 Ride straight through the stop sign; then turn left onto Whitneyville Road.

★   5.9 Turn left onto 52nd Street.

★   12.3 Turn right onto Pratt Lake Avenue.

★   14.7 Turn left onto 64th Street.

　 15.7 Ride onto Drew Road.

★   17.7 Turn right onto Bell Road.

★   18.1 Turn left onto Clarksville Road.

★   20.1 Clarksville. Turn left onto Nash Highway.

★   23.0 Turn left onto Grand River Avenue.

★   25.5 Turn right onto Hastings Road.

★   26.3 Turn left onto Peck Lake Road.

★   26.5 Turn right onto Conklin Road.

★   27.3 Turn left onto Ware Road.

★   27.6 Turn right onto Oberley Drive.

★ 28.7 Turn right onto Grand River Drive, which becomes Division Street.
★ 29.3 Turn left onto Main Street. Lowell.
★ 29.8 Turn left onto South Hudson Street.
★ 30.5 Turn right onto Grand River Avenue.
★ 40.5 Turn right onto Buttrick Avenue.
★ 41.2 Turn left onto Fase Street.
   41.5 Covered bridge in Ada. End of ride.

Ludington Trek
Submitted by Laurie James

This relaxing ride across both flat and rolling terrain takes you along the Hart-Montague Bicycle Trail.

Type of ride: road bike
Starting point: Montague
Finishing point: Ludington
Distance: 47 miles
Level of difficulty: moderate
General terrain: mostly flat, with rolling hills toward the end
Traffic conditions: mostly low-volume, two-lane roads and bike paths
Estimated riding time: 3 hours
Best season/time of day to ride: spring through fall
Points of interest: fruit orchards; tree-lined sections; pretty views; campgrounds; White Pine Village Historic Museum
Accommodations and services: Hart-Montague Bicycle Trail is a state park and requires a pass to use; passes available from merchants in Montague or from a ranger along the ride
Supplemental maps or other information: A free trail map is available from Silver Lake State Park, (616) 873-3083

GETTING THERE
Take US 31 north from Muskegon to Fruitvale Road. Turn west and follow the road 0.25 mile to the four-way stop. Turn south onto Oceana Drive and go to its end at Hart-Montague State Park.

Ludington Hydroelectric Plant (photo by: Laurie James)

IN THE SADDLE

Head north on the Hart-Montague Bicycle Trail for 1.5 miles, until you reach the point where it crosses Fruitvale Road on the way to Rothbury. The scenery is mostly oak trees and ferns as the trail runs parallel to Oceana Dive. The route passes along the outskirts of several towns, making side trips feasible but not requiring a trip down the main streets.

At mile 5.9, the route crosses Winston Road in Rothbury and begins a transition into more agricultural areas about 3 miles later. Look for asparagus fields on the left and corn fields on the right. The Oceana County asparagus festival is the first weekend in June.

After passing through the town of New Era and crossing M20, the trail crosses its first railroad trestle and passes the Country Dairy Show Barn. This also begins a section that includes many fruit orchards. Crossing the second railroad bridge, the trail transitions to a section with less traffic and many "tunnels" formed by trees.

Leave the off-road portion of the trail at Mears (mile 19.5) and turn left (north) onto 55th Avenue. A short distance farther is a four-way stop at Fox Road. Turn left onto Fox Road and pass through the village, which offers views of the Silver Lake Sand Dunes.

At mile 22.5, turn right onto Wilson Avenue; a mile farther, turn left onto Deer Road and then right onto 34th Avenue, which becomes

B15. In less than a mile, you will turn right onto Ridge Avenue and then bear right onto Long Bridge Road at just over the 30-mile point. This road will take you along the south edge of Pentwater Lake and across Long Bridge. Turn left onto Business US 31 at 31.2 miles.

The highway leads to Pentwater, which has a marina and a state park within a few blocks of downtown. There are two campgrounds as you leave the town. Continue on the route to mile 37.5 at the Wishing Well Gas Station. Turn north for the last time onto Lakeshore Drive. The road is a little rough as it winds around Bass Lake, and it begins picking up some hills around mile 40. At mile 44, the road crosses the grounds of the Ludington Hydro-electric Plant.

Continue past the White Pine Village Historic Museum and conclude the ride at Buttersville Park, located on the south side of the channel in Ludington. This town, at the mouth of the Père Marquette River, is one of Michigan's most important shipping points. It borders both Lake Michigan and Père Marquette Lake. The latter provides a safe harbor for passenger boats and car ferries. The town was named for James Ludington, a lumberman who operated here in the 1880s.

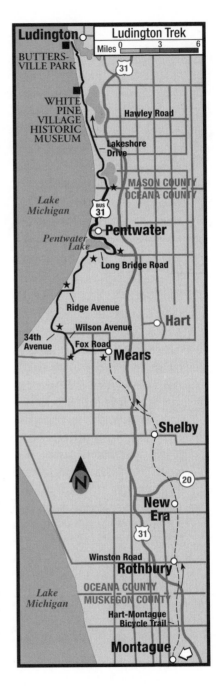

RIDE GUIDE

    0.0 From the trailhead in Montague, ride north on the Hart-Montague Bicycle Trail.

    5.9 Cross Winston Road.

    9.4 New Era.

    10.5 Cross M20.

    11.1 Country Dairy Show Barn.

★ 19.5 At Mears, turn left onto 55th Avenue.

★ 19.7 Turn left onto Fox Road.

★ 22.5 Turn right onto Wilson Avenue.

★ 23.3 Turn left onto Deer Road and then right onto 34th Avenue.

★ 24.0 Turn right onto Ridge Avenue.

★ 30.1 Bear right onto Long Bridge Road.

★ 31.2 Turn left onto Business US 31.

    34.1 Pentwater.

★ 37.5 Turn left onto Lakeshore Drive.

    40.8 Summit Park.

    46.3 White Pine Village Historic Museum.

    47.0 Buttersville Park. End of ride.

Country Dairy Show Barn (photo by: Laurie James)

Lake Michigan Trek

26 *Submitted by Vern Cascaddan*

This week-long ride follows the route of the League of Michigan Bicyclists' Shoreline West Bicycle Tour. Outstanding beaches and picturesque marinas are regularly encountered along the entire route.

Type of ride: road bike
Starting point: Holland
Finishing point: the Mackinac Bridge in Mackinaw City
Distance: 387.3 miles, one way
Level of difficulty: moderate
General terrain: rolling to hilly
Traffic conditions: ride follows mostly low-volume, two-lane roads
Estimated riding time: 7 days
Best season/time of day to ride: mid-June through mid-September; best to start on Sunday and finish on Sunday
Points of interest: The route passes numerous beaches and state parks. Many of the small towns along the way are old lumber settlements that have made the transition into harbors of refuge for artists and tourists. Sleeping Bear Dunes National Lakeshore is situated along the route on day 4, outside the town of Empire.
Accommodations and services: plenty of camping and other services along the route; bike shops include the Highwheeler in Holland at 211 S. River Avenue
Supplemental maps or other information: Shoreline West Bicycle Tour pamphlet available from the League of Michigan Bicyclists, P.O. Box 16201, Lansing, MI 48901

GETTING THERE
Park near the school in Holland on Riley Street, between 136th and 140th. Begin riding here.

IN THE SADDLE
This week-long ride leads along the shore of Lake Michigan to the Straits of Mackinac, passing through lakeside villages and some of the very best scenery the Wolverine State has to offer. The route is divided into seven days, with mileages of 51, 39, 45, 63, 75, 44, and 70. (Please

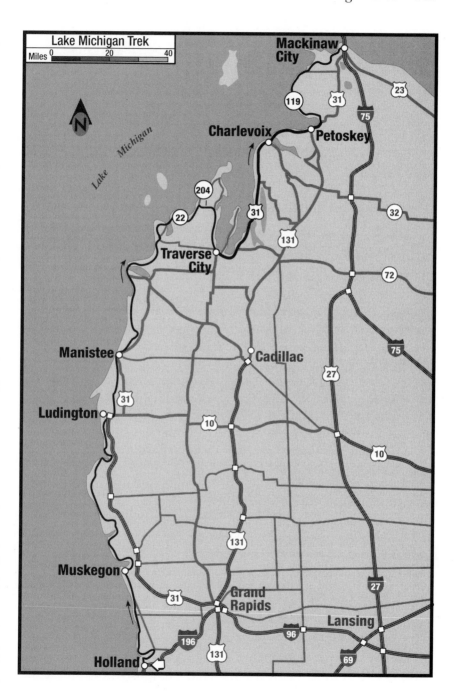

note that if you are planning to camp, you will need to divide the route up differently than we have done here, because on the organized tour participants stay overnight in public schools.)

Day 1

The 51-mile route followed on Day 1 traces the shore of Lake Michigan, skirting a selection of inviting beaches. State parks at Grand Haven and Muskegon offer camping. The day ends at Muskegon State Park.

From the school, turn right (west) onto Riley Street, go 0.2 mile, and turn right onto 140th Avenue. Turn left onto Quincy Street at 1.2 miles; then, at mile 5.4, turn right onto Lake Shore Avenue. At mile 9.6, bear left to continue on Lake Shore, as Butternut merges from the right. Pass Kirk Park at 13.2 miles. At mile 17.0, cross Lincoln.

At 20 miles, cross Robbins Road, enter Grand Haven, and turn left at mile 20.3 onto Grand Avenue. Turn right onto South Harbor Drive and ride into Grand Haven State Park at 21.1 miles.From the park ride onto Jackson Street and at 23.6 miles, turn left onto US 31. Exercise great caution here and at mile 24.3 as you cross the Spring Lake exit. Bear right off US 31 at mile 24.4 at the Ferrysburg exit; then turn left onto 3rd Street. Go right onto 174th Street at mile 24.7; then turn left onto Dogwood Drive, passing a store at 25.3 miles. At 26.6 miles, turn right onto 180th Street and then left onto Hickory Street at 27.2 miles. Turn right onto Palm Street at 27.7 miles and right onto Black Lake Road at 28.4 miles. Go left onto Pontaluma Road at 29.4. Bear right at mile 30.1 onto Lake Harbor Road (Hoffmaster State Park).

Turn left onto Norton Avenue at 34.6 miles and right onto Lincoln Road at 35.4 miles. Turn left onto Sherman Street at 36.5 and then right onto Beach Street at 37.3 miles. Turn left onto the bike path at 37.7 miles and then right onto Lakeshore Drive at 38.3 miles. At 40.0 miles is Lakeside, where you will find services, including groceries. Bear left to continue on Lakeshore Drive at 40.6 miles, right onto Michigan at 41.3 miles, left onto Franklin Road at 41.5 miles, right onto Western Avenue at 41.6 miles, and left onto 4th Street at 42.4 miles. Go right onto Terrace Street at mile 42.5, left onto Western Avenue at mile 43.1, right onto Eastern Avenue at mile 43.4, left onto Ottawa Street at mile 43.5, right onto Bayou Avenue at mile 44.2, and left onto Seaway/US Business 31 at mile 44.3. At mile 44.5, cautiously bear left at the

"Spiderweb." Cross the Muskegon River at 45.5 miles and M120 at 45.8 miles. Turn left onto Ruddiman Drive at 46.0 miles. At 49 miles, cross Bear Lake (food), and at 51.1 miles enter Muskegon State Park.

Day 2

Today's 39-mile ride continues along the shore of Lake Michigan. At mile 52.1, turn right onto Scenic Drive, go 9.8 miles and turn right onto South Shore Drive. Bear left onto South Lake Street at mile 64.0 and ride into Whitehall. At mile 67.4 turn right onto River Street, and then immediately turn left onto US Business 31. Turn left at mile 68.2 and ride into Montague. At mile 68.5 bear right onto School Street, and then immediately turn right onto Stanton Street.

At mile 69.2 turn onto the Hart-Montague Bicycle Trail, the first state park rail-trail with an improved surface. Since this is a state park it requires a user pass. Trail passes are a major source of revenue for trail operations; these passes can be purchased at various businesses in the communities along the route, or from park rangers patrolling the trail. Individual passes are $2 and annual passes are $10.

The trail makes a beeline north heading for Rothbury at mile 75.2. In Rothbury a side trail leads to a local park which has a picnic area, a playground, and restrooms. The trail continues north to the town of New Era, where there is another trailside park with a covered pavilion, restrooms, and a small creek. There is also a smaller trail that leads to an ice cream parlor.

From New Era the trail travels through Shelby and on to Mears. The stretch between Shelby and Mears has been called the trail's most scenic part. There are two rest stops on this stretch; the newest one overlooks East Golden Pond.

Just before Hart, at mile 90.2, turn left onto 72nd Avenue heading toward Pentwater.

Day 3

Today's 45-mile journey will take you through the towns of Pentwater, home of the famous Antler Bar, and Ludington, which is well known for its great beach and long public pier. You will end your day on the outskirts of Manistee.

Continue on 72nd Avenue to mile 95.2, and turn left onto Monroe Road. At mile 101.0 turn left onto Madison Road and then ride onto

US Business 31. Ride through the town of Pentwater and then at mile 104.1, bear left onto Lake Shore Drive and ride along the Lake Michigan shoreline.

Turn right onto Iris Road at mile 109.1 and then, at mile 110.6, turn left onto Père Marquette Road. Ride for 0.9 mile and turn left onto 6th Street and ride into Ludington. Situated at the mouth of the Père Marquette River, Ludington is a popular fishing center and port on the eastern shore of Lake Michigan. Père Marquette Lake, around which you will ride, is a safe deepwater harborage for freighters and pleasure craft.

At mile 113.0 turn right onto Washington Street and then in 1.5 miles turn left onto Bryant Street. Ride 1 mile and then turn right onto Lake Shore Drive. At mile 118.1 turn right onto Nell Road, and then immediately turn left onto Stearns Road. Turn right onto Dewey Road in 0.4 miles and then at mile 120.3, turn left onto Jebavy Drive. At mile 120.5 turn right onto Angling Road and then right onto Victory Drive at mile 121.7. Turn left onto Stiles Road at mile 124.8, and then a quick jog right onto Town Line Road before turning left onto Quarterline Road at mile 128.3. Ride to mile 134.9 and turn right onto County Line Road, and then in 0.2 miles turn left onto Maple Road and ride into the outskirts of Manistee.

Day 4

Today's 63-mile ride, hillier and even more scenic than the previous leg, passes through Frankfort, an area famous among glider enthusiasts for its favorable winds. Not far from Frankfort is the Point Betsie Lighthouse, a popular subject for photographers, which dates from before the Civil War.

Continue on Maple Road to mile 140.5 and ride across the bridge onto Washington Street into Manistee. Manistee's name means "spirit of the woods," and in the nineteenth century, the town's major industry was logging; every year in July the National Forest Festival is held here. Today it is a shipping point for the annual deluge of fruit grown in the area.

At mile 141.0 turn right onto Monroe Street and then in 0.2 miles turn left onto US 31. In 0.6 miles, turn left onto M110 and then right onto Lakeshore Road. Follow the shoreline to Portage Lake and mile 149.1, where you will ride onto Crescent Beach Road. At mile 150.2, turn left onto M22 and ride through the town of Onekama.

Follow M22 through the towns of Arcadia and Elberta and then on into Frankfort. Just before Frankfort, at mile 174.4, bear right onto the bridge to continue on M22. At mile 175.3, turn left onto Main Street and ride into downtown Frankfort. People are drawn to the town for its sandy beaches, natural harbor, and boat-launching ramp.

At mile 175.6 turn right onto 10th Street and then in 0.3 mile, turn left onto James Street. Turn right onto M22 at mile 176.1 and follow it around Crystal, Platte, and Little Platte Lakes. Continue riding on M22 to mile 197.3 where you take a left onto Wilco Road. At mile 198.4 turn right onto Front Street in downtown Empire.

Day 5

This area of the state offers many attractions, including the Cherry Capital of the World, Traverse City, which annually produces some 100 million pounds of cherries, numerous wineries, and the famous Sleeping Bear Dunes. Because there is so much to see, you may want to break this 75-mile portion of the tour into two days.

In Empire turn left onto M22 and ride for just under two miles before bearing left onto M109. At mile 205.6 turn right to continue on

Michigan's renowned tart cherries (photo by: Jim DuFresne)

M109. After 5.5 miles ride onto M22. At mile 215.8 turn left onto North Traverse Lake Road and ride for 0.3 miles before turning left onto M22.

At mile 224.0 ride into Lake Leelanau, which is fast becoming a wine-producing area, due to the area's favorable climate and soil conditions. Continue riding north on M22 until mile 224.2 where you will turn right onto M204. At mile 231.4 turn right onto St. Mary's Street and ride for 0.5 miles before turning right onto Broadway Avenue. Just after riding onto Broadway look for Elm Street on your left and take that turn.

Ride onto County Road 633 at mile 232.2 and continue for just under 10 miles before bearing left on County Road 633/614. At mile 245.8 turn right onto M22, then right onto M72 at mile 247.0. Look for Bay Street on your left and take it, followed by a quick left onto the TART bike path. Take this path all the way through Traverse City.

With its setting at the head of Grand Traverse Bay, Traverse City is a busy resort town in all seasons. There is cross-country skiing in the winter and good sailing and fishing in the summer, and the city is also host to some of the biggest mountain bike races in the country. It is said that almost one-third of the world's cherry crop is produced here, an industry that grew from a one-acre plot planted in 1880. The National Cherry Festival is held here every July.

The TART trail is Michigan's only "rails with trails" trail, meaning that it is located close to an active rail line. The trail is expanding each year and is becoming a vital part of the alternative transportation scene in Traverse City.

At the end of the TART trail, at mile 256.1, turn right onto Bunker Hill Road. At mile 257.7 turn left onto Lautner Street, then in 2 miles turn right onto Brackett Road. At 261.3 turn left onto Saylor Road, followed by a right onto Yuba and another left onto Bates Road. Turn right onto Angell Drive at mile 264.8, then left onto Munro Road at mile 266.8. Two miles later turn right onto Town Line Road, followed in 0.5 miles by a left onto Elk Lake Road. At mile 271.2 turn right onto Green Road, followed immediately by a left onto 4th Street and a right onto Bridge Street. At mile 272.0 turn left onto River Street and then immediately right onto Dexter Street. Just under a mile afterwards, turn right onto Rivershore Drive and then left onto Ames Street at mile 273.3. Ride through downtown Elk Rapids before turning right at mile 273.7 onto North Bayshore Road.

Day 6

Torch Lake, lined with big, beautiful homes, highlights today's 44-mile ride. You will also visit Charlevoix, a charming town with countless shops and eateries. This route is particularly beautiful in the spring, when the roadside meadows are blanketed with wildflowers.

Continue riding on North Bayshore Road before turning right onto Williams Drive at mile 276.1. At mile 277.2 turn left onto Cairn Street and ride for 0.5 miles before turning left to continue on Cairn/Cherry Street. In 0.2 miles turn right onto Indian Road and follow this for just over 2 miles before turning left and riding along the shoreline of Torch Lake on West Torch Lake Drive.

At mile 288.0 turn left onto Barnes Road before taking a right onto US 31 (Cairn Highway) at mile 288.9. After passing through Eastport, turn left onto Lore Road and then immediately right onto Old Dixie Highway at mile 295.3. At 301.9 turn left onto Genett Road, followed by a right onto 4th Street/Norwood Road at mile 302.3. At mile 311.4 turn left onto US 31 again and ride for just under 0.5 miles before turning right onto Stover Road.

At mile 312.7 turn left onto Ferry Avenue and ride north along the shoreline of Lake Charlevoix. Turn left onto Belvedere Avenue followed by a right onto US 31 and ride into downtown Charlevoix. This town is one of the premier resort centers in the state, with Lake Michigan to the west and Lake Charlevoix to the east. There are excellent boating opportunities and many nice beaches in the area. The city offers concerts in the town bandshell during the months of July and August.

Just outside of Charlevoix, turn right onto Dixon Road, followed by a left onto Mercer Boulevard at mile 315.3. One mile farther, turn right onto Waller Road at 316.3, and then left back onto US 31 at mile 317.4.

Day 7

This 70-mile ride is a fitting finale to this great seven-day outing—from the great old homes of Harbor Springs, which has been a popular resort since the turn of the century, to the impressive sight of the Mackinac Bridge rising on the horizon at day's end.

Continue on US 31, then turn right onto Murray Road at mile 323.7. At mile 324.6 turn left onto Upper Bayshore Road, then left onto Pin Cherry. At mile 328.7 turn right onto Townsend Road, followed by two quick lefts onto Kiebel Road and Lake Grove Drive. After a right onto Intertown Road at mile 330.8, turn left onto Eppler Road and right onto Sheridan and ride into Petoskey.

Petoskey is another resort center, located on Little Traverse Bay. There are three major ski developments and fourteen public golf courses within 30 miles of the city. The city's most interesting monument is a life-size figure of Christ that is located in the bay, 30 feet below the surface, which serves as a skin divers' shrine. In June, the Little Traverse Bay Historic Festival features antiques, parades, and craft demonstrations.

Outside of town ride onto Mitchell Road and at mile 337.8 turn left onto Division Road. Turn right onto US 31 at mile 338.7 and left onto M119 at mile 339.3. At mile 341.3 turn left onto Beach Road and left again onto Fern Avenue at mile 343.1 to follow a less crowded, more scenic route along the bay. At mile 343.7 turn left to rejoin Beach Road, then turn right onto Zoll at mile 344.9.

Zoll will take you into downtown Harbor Springs. At mile 345.0 turn left onto Bay Street, then right onto State Street and left onto M119

Lining up to eat (photo by: Vern Cascaddan)

to ride out of Harbor Springs. At mile 349.2, turn left onto Lower Shore Drive to continue on the scenic ride up the shoreline of Lake Michigan. Turn left onto M119 (Lake Shore Drive) again at mile 352.8 and enjoy the ride up the coastline.

Pass through the towns of Good Hart and Cross Village before turning away from Lake Michigan on Sturgeon Bay Trail. At mile 371.5 turn left onto West Bliss Road, followed by a right onto Gill Road at mile 372.4. Turn left onto Cecil Bay Road at mile 379.5 and then right onto Wilderness Park Drive at mile 381.4.

At mile 384.9, turn left and then right onto County Road 81, which eventually becomes West Central Avenue. This will take you into downtown Mackinaw City and the end of the ride.

RIDE GUIDE

Day 1

★   0.0 From the school parking lot in Holland, turn right onto Riley Street.

★   0.2 Turn right onto 140th Avenue.

★   1.2 Turn left onto Quincy Street.

★   5.4 Turn right onto Lake Shore Avenue.

   9.6 Bear left to continue on Lake Shore Avenue.

   10.7 Campbell Power Plant.

   13.2 Pass Kirk Park.

★   20.3 Turn left onto Grand Avenue.

★   21.1 Turn right onto South Harbor Drive and ride into Grand Haven State Park.

   22.9 Ride onto Jackson St.

★   23.6 Turn left onto US 31.

   24.4 Bear right onto Ferrysburg exit.

★   24.5 Turn left onto 3rd Street.

★   24.7 Turn right onto 174th Street.

★   25.3 Turn left onto Dogwood Drive.

★   26.6 Turn right onto 180th Street.

★   27.2 Turn left onto Hickory Street.

★   27.7 Turn right onto Palm Street.

★   28.4 Turn right onto Black Lake Road.

★   29.4 Turn left onto Pontaluma Road.

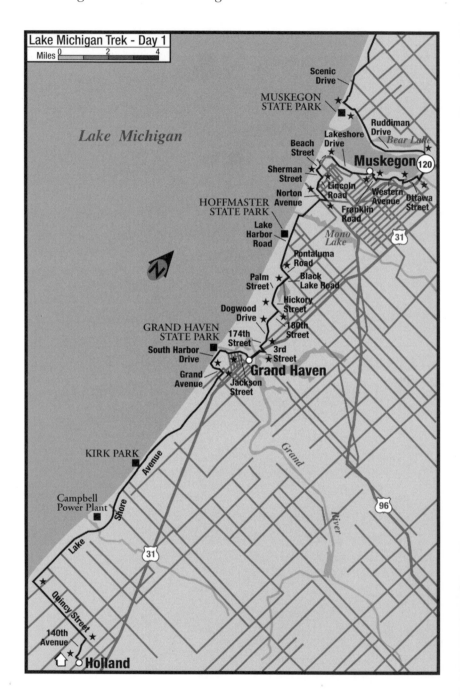

Lake Michigan Trek - Day 1
Miles 0   2   4

★ 30.1 Bear right onto Lake Harbor Road.
★ 34.6 Turn left on Norton Avenue.
★ 35.4 Turn right onto Lincoln Road.
★ 36.5 Turn left onto Sherman Street.
★ 37.3 Turn right onto Beach Street.
★ 37.7 Turn left onto bike path.
★ 38.3 Turn right onto Lakeshore Drive.
★ 40.6 Bear left and continue on Lakeshore Drive.
★ 41.3 Turn right onto Michigan.
★ 41.5 Turn left onto Franklin Road.
★ 41.6 Turn right onto Western Avenue.
★ 42.4 Turn left onto 4th Street.
★ 42.5 Turn right onto Terrace Street.
★ 43.1 Turn left onto Western Avenue.
★ 43.4 Turn right onto Eastern Avenue.
★ 43.5 Turn left onto Ottawa Street.
★ 44.2 Turn right onto Bayou Avenue.
★ 44.3 Turn left onto Seaway/US Business 31.
★ 44.5 Bear left at the "Spiderweb."
   45.8 Cross M120.
★ 46.0 Turn left onto Ruddiman Drive.
★ 51.1 Enter Muskegon State Park.

Day 2
★ 52.1 Turn right onto Scenic Drive.
★ 61.9 Turn right onto South Shore Drive.
★ 64.0 Bear left onto South Lake Street.
★ 67.4 Turn right onto River Street.
★ 67.5 Turn left onto US Business 31.
★ 68.2 Turn left onto Hunt.
★ 68.5 Bear right onto School Street.
★ 68.6 Turn right onto Stanton Street.
★ 69.2 Turn onto Hart-Montague Bicycle Trail.
   75.2 Rothbury.
   78.8 New Era.
   82.9 Shelby.
   88.8 Mears.
★ 90.2 Turn left onto 72nd Avenue.

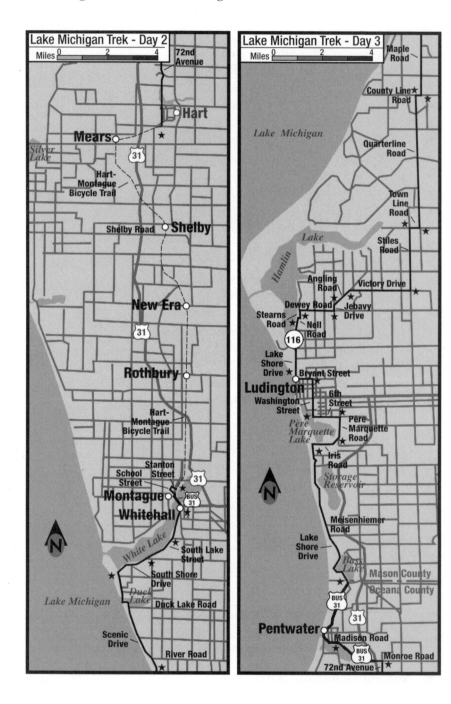

Day 3

★   95.2 Turn left onto Monroe Road.
★ 101.0 Turn left onto Madison Road.
★ 101.2 Ride onto US Business 31.
    101.4 Pentwater.
★ 104.1 Bear left onto Lake Shore Drive.
★ 109.1 Turn right onto Iris Road.
★ 110.6 Turn left onto Père Marquette Road.
★ 111.7 Turn left onto 6th Street.
★ 113.0 Turn right onto Washington Street.
★ 114.5 Turn left onto Bryant Street.
★ 115.5 Turn right onto Lake Shore Drive.
    116.9 Bear right to continue on Lake Shore Drive.
★ 118.1 Turn right onto Nell Road.
★ 118.2 Turn left onto Stearns Road.
★ 118.6 Turn right onto Dewey Road.
★ 120.3 Turn left onto Jebavy Drive.
★ 120.5 Turn right onto Angling Road.
★ 121.7 Turn right onto Victory Drive.
★ 124.8 Turn left onto Stiles Road.
★ 127.9 Turn right onto Town Line Road.
★ 128.3 Turn left onto Quarterline Road.
★ 134.9 Turn right onto County Line Road.
★ 135.1 Turn left onto Maple Road.

Day 4

★ 140.5 Ride across bridge and onto Washington Street.
★ 141.0 Turn right onto Monroe Street.
★ 141.2 Turn left onto US 31.
★ 141.8 Turn left onto M110.
★ 141.0 Turn right onto Lakeshore Road.
★ 149.1 Ride onto Crescent Beach Road.
★ 150.2 Turn left onto M22.
    152.2 Onekama.
    162.4 Arcadia.
    174.2 Elberta.
★ 174.4 Bear right onto bridge to continue on M22.
★ 175.3 Turn left onto Main Street. Frankfort.

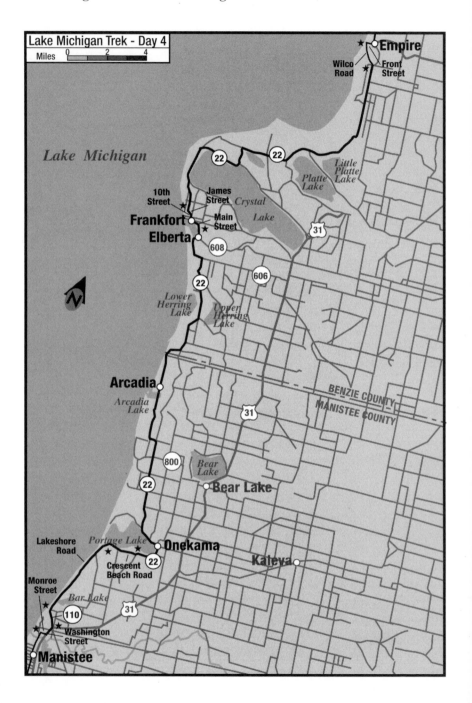

Lake Michigan Trek - Day 4

Miles 0   2   4

Empire
Wilco Road
Front Street

Lake Michigan

22   22

Little Platte Lake

Platte Lake

10th Street
James Street
Crystal Lake

Frankfort
Main Street
Elberta
608
31

22
606

Lower Herring Lake
Upper Herring Lake

Arcadia
Arcadia Lake

BENZIE COUNTY
MANISTEE COUNTY

31

800
Bear Lake

22
Bear Lake

Kaleva

Lakeshore Road
Portage Lake
Onekama
22
Crescent Beach Road

Monroe Street
Bar Lake
31

110
Washington Street

Manistee

★ 175.6 Turn right onto 10th Street.
★ 175.9 Turn left onto James Street.
★ 176.1 Turn right onto M22.
★ 197.3 Turn left onto Wilco Road.
★ 198.4 Turn right onto Front Street. Empire.

Day 5

★ 198.6 Turn left onto M22.
★ 200.7 Turn left onto M109.
★ 205.6 Turn right and continue on M109.
★ 211.1 Ride onto M22.
★ 215.8 Turn left onto North Traverse Lake Road.
★ 218.8 Turn left onto M22.
★ 224.2 Turn right onto M204.
★ 231.4 Turn right onto St. Mary's Street.
★ 231.9 Turn right onto Broadway Avenue.
★ 232.0 Turn left onto Elm Street.
★ 232.2 Ride onto County Road 633.
★ 242.8 Turn left onto County Road 633/614.
★ 245.8 Turn right onto M22.
★ 247.0 Turn right onto M72.
★ 247.1 Turn left onto Bay Steet and then left onto TART bike path.
★ 256.1 Turn right onto Bunker Hill Road.
★ 257.7 Turn left onto Lautner Street.
★ 259.7 Turn right onto Bracket Road.
★ 261.3 Turn left onto Saylor Road.
★ 263.3 Turn right onto Yuba Street.
★ 263.8 Turn left onto Bates Road.
★ 264.8 Turn right onto Angell Drive.
★ 266.8 Turn left onto Munro Road.
★ 268.8 Turn right onto Town Line Road.
★ 269.3 Turn left onto Elk Lake Road.
★ 271.2 Turn right onto Green Road.
★ 271.3 Turn left onto 4th Street.
★ 271.4 Turn right onto Bridge Street.
★ 272.0 Turn left onto River Street and then immediately right onto Dexter Street.
★ 272.9 Turn right onto Rivershore Drive.

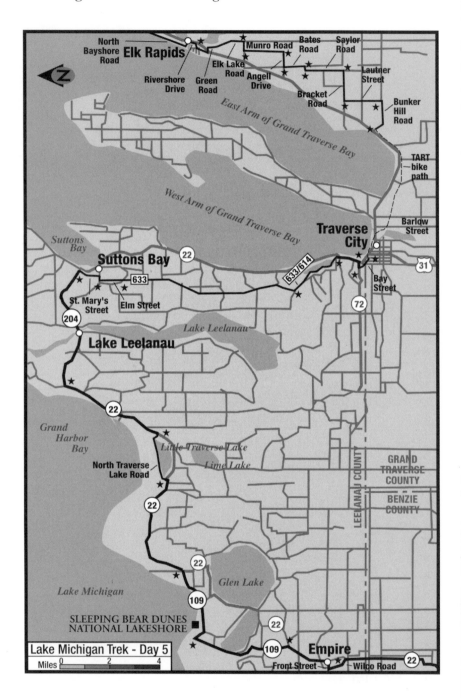

North Bayshore Road

Elk Rapids

Munro Road

Bates Road

Saylor Road

Rivershore Drive

Elk Lake Road

Green Road

Angell Drive

Lautner Street

Bracket Road

Bunker Hill Road

East Arm of Grand Traverse Bay

TART bike path

West Arm of Grand Traverse Bay

Barlow Street

Traverse City

Suttons Bay

Suttons Bay

22

633

633/614

31

St. Mary's Street

Elm Street

Bay Street

72

204

Lake Leelanau

Lake Leelanau

Grand Harbor Bay

22

Little Traverse Lake

Lime Lake

North Traverse Lake Road

GRAND TRAVERSE COUNTY

22

LEELANAU COUNTY

BENZIE COUNTY

Lake Michigan

22

22

109

Glen Lake

SLEEPING BEAR DUNES NATIONAL LAKESHORE

22

109

Empire

Front Street

Wilco Road

22

Lake Michigan Trek - Day 5

Miles 0   2   4

★ 273.3 Turn left onto Ames Street.
★ 273.7 Turn right onto North Bayshore Road.

Day 6
★ 276.1 Turn right onto Williams Drive.
★ 277.2 Turn left onto Cairn Street.
★ 277.7 Turn left to continue on Cairn/Cherry Street.
★ 277.9 Turn right onto Indian Road.
★ 280.1 Turn left onto West Torch Lake Drive.
★ 288.0 Turn left onto Barnes Road.
★ 288.9 Turn right onto US 31 (Cairn Highway).
★ 295.3 Turn left onto Lore Road and then immediately right onto Old Dixie Highway.
★ 301.9 Turn left onto Genett Road.
★ 302.3 Turn right onto 4th Street/Norwood Road.
★ 311.4 Turn left onto US 31.
★ 311.8 Turn right onto Stover Road.
★ 312.0 Turn left to continue on Stover Road.
★ 312.7 Turn left onto Ferry Avenue.
★ 313.6 Turn left onto Belvedere Avenue.
★ 314.2 Turn right onto US 31.
★ 314.6 Turn right onto Dixon Road.
★ 315.3 Turn left onto Mercer Boulevard.
★ 316.3 Turn right onto Waller Road.
★ 317.4 Turn left onto US 31.

Day 7
★ 323.7 Turn right onto Murray Road.
★ 324.6 Turn left onto Upper Bayshore Road.
★ 325.0 Turn left onto Pin Cherry.
★ 328.7 Turn right onto Townsend Road.
★ 330.0 Turn left onto Kiebel Road.
★ 330.5 Turn left onto Lake Grove Drive.
★ 330.8 Turn right onto Intertown Road.
★ 332.8 Turn left onto Eppler Road.
★ 334.3 Turn right onto Sheridan Road. Petoskey.
★ 335.8 Turn left onto Howard Street.
★ 335.9 Turn right onto Jennings Street.

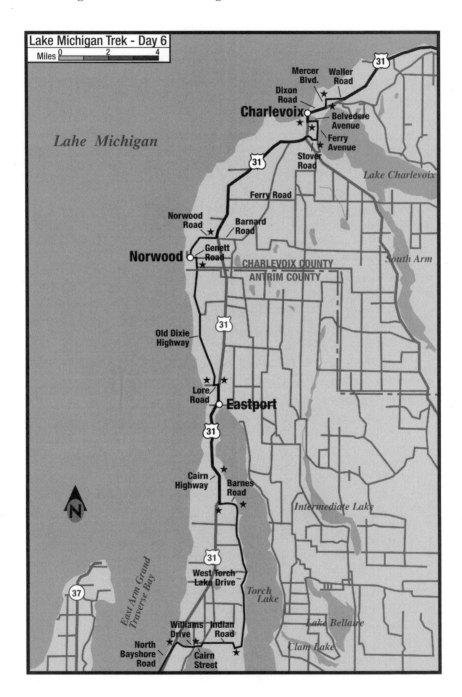

Lake Michigan Trek - Day 6

Miles 0   2   4

31

Mercer Blvd.   Waller Road

Dixon Road

Charlevoix   Belvedere Avenue

Lahe Michigan   Ferry Avenue

31   Stover Road

Lake Charlevoix

Ferry Road

Norwood Road   Barnard Road

Norwood   Genett Road

CHARLEVOIX COUNTY   *South Arm*

ANTRIM COUNTY

31

Old Dixie Highway

Lore Road   **Eastport**

31

Cairn Highway   Barnes Road

Intermediate Lake

31

West Torch Lake Drive   *Torch Lake*

37

Williams Drive   Indian Road   *Lake Bellaire*

North Bayshore Road   Cairn Street   *Clam Lake*

East Arm Grand Traverse Bay

N

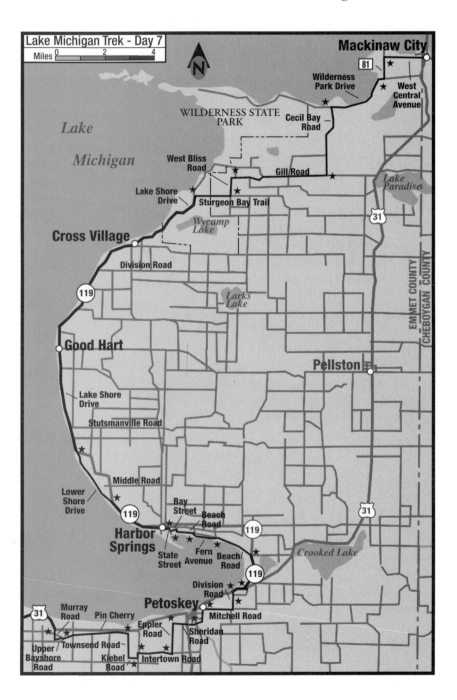

Lake Michigan Trek - Day 7
Miles 0 2 4

N

Mackinaw City
81
West Central Avenue
Wilderness Park Drive
Cecil Bay Road
WILDERNESS STATE PARK
Lake Michigan
West Bliss Road
Gill Road
Lake Paradise
Lake Shore Drive
Sturgeon Bay Trail
31
Wycamp Lake
Cross Village
Division Road
Larks Lake
119
Good Hart
Pellston
Lake Shore Drive
EMMET COUNTY
CHEBOYGAN COUNTY
Stutsmanville Road
Middle Road
Lower Shore Drive
119
Bay Street
Beach Road
119
31
Harbor Springs
State Street
Fern Avenue
Beach/Road
Crooked Lake
119
Division Road
Petoskey
Mitchell Road
31
Murray Road
Pin Cherry
Eppler Road
Sheridan Road
Upper Bayshore Road
Townsend Road
Kiebel Road
Intertown Road

★ 337.3 Turn right onto Mitchell Road.
★ 337.8 Turn left onto Division Road.
★ 338.7 Turn right onto US 31.
★ 339.3 Turn left onto M119.
★ 341.3 Turn left onto Beach Road.
★ 343.1 Turn left onto Fern Avenue.
★ 343.7 Turn left onto Beach Road.
★ 344.0 Turn left to continue on Beach Road.
★ 344.9 Turn right onto Zoll.
★ 345.0 Harbor Springs. Turn left onto Bay Street.
★ 345.5 Turn right onto State Street.
★ 345.8 Turn left onto M119.
★ 349.2 Turn left onto Lower Shore Drive.
★ 352.8 Turn left onto M119 (Lake Shore Drive).
   359.2 Good Hart.
   367.4 Cross Village.
★ 370.3 Turn right onto Sturgeon Bay Trail.
★ 371.5 Turn left onto West Bliss Road.
★ 372.4 Turn right onto Gill Road.
★ 379.5 Turn left onto Cecil Bay Road.
★ 381.4 Turn right onto Wilderness Park Drive.
★ 384.9 Turn left onto County Road 81.
★ 385.9 Turn right onto County Road 81, which becomes West
         Central Avenue.
★ 387.3 Mackinaw City. End of ride.

27 Kal-Haven Trail
Submitted by Michael F. Sproul

The Kal-Haven Trail Sesquicentennial State Park is a multi-use
recreational park following the abandoned right-of-way of the Penn
Central/New York Central rail line.

Type of ride: mountain bike advised, but road bike okay on the hard-
   packed, crushed limestone surface
Starting point: Blue Star Highway trailhead in South Haven

Finishing point: 10th Street trailhead in Oshtemo Township, near the city of Kalamazoo

Distance: 33.5 miles

Level of difficulty: easy

General terrain: flat railroad grade

Traffic conditions: none

Estimated riding time: 3 to 4 hours

Best season/time of day to ride: summer and fall, any day of the week

Points of interest: South Haven boasts the Michigan Maritime Museum, situated on Dyckman Avenue at the Black River Bridge. The museum highlights the long and colorful history of navigation on Lake Michigan. Call (616) 637-8078 for information. The most popular attraction at the other end of the trail is the Kalamazoo Aviation History Museum, located at 3101 East Milham Road, (616) 382-6555. World War II fighters, as well as vintage uniforms and other aircraft and memorabilia are on display. A highlight on the trail is the high trestle spanning the Black River, which has been converted into a covered bridge.

Accommodations and services: Numerous water and picnic stops are located along the trail, with convenience stores and restaurants in several small towns along the route. The resort town of South Haven has lodging, private camping, restaurants, and a public beach. South of town is Van Buren State Park, with beach facilities, picnicking, and camping. Kalamazoo offers all services, including bike shops.

Supplemental maps or other information: available through Kal-Haven Trail State Park, 23960 Ruggles Road, South Haven, MI 49090, (616) 637-4984

GETTING THERE

The trailhead for the Kal-Haven Trail is located north of South Haven off the Blue Star Highway, which is parallel to and just west of I-196, just south of the Allegan–Van Buren county line (Baseline Road). Watch for the trailhead where you cross the Black River.

IN THE SADDLE

The Kal-Haven Trail passes through numerous towns and villages, crosses several bridges, and encounters many points of historical

The Black River covered bridge (photo by: Michael Sproul)

interest as it traverses some of Michigan's most attractive countryside. South Haven is an important Michigan port and is the supply city for a number of surrounding resorts, many of them built around the forty inland lakes that lie within a 20-mile radius of the city.

From the Blue Star trailhead, ride east onto the Kal-Haven Trail, crossing the Black River at 0.4 mile via a covered bridge. At mile 1.5, pass the first of many blueberry farms you will see between here and Grand Junction, which, not incidentally, is nicknamed the "Blueberry Capital of Michigan." The horse trail that parallels the biking/hiking trail begins here at mile 3 and continues for several miles. Picnic tables and a water pump are available at 3.4 miles and again at 7 miles (from the latter point, a public phone can be found just south of the nearby antique shop in Lacota).

Cross Barber Creek at 11 miles on old Camel Back Bridge, once used to carry vehicles over passing trains. Lake Eleven is just 0.3 mile north of the trail at the 13-mile point. The horse trail ends at mile 15.8 in Bloomingdale; just beyond is the Country Pub, with its unusual ceiling display of thirty beehives (all inactive, one hopes). Bloomingdale also has a deli, a convenience store, and a restored depot now serving as a

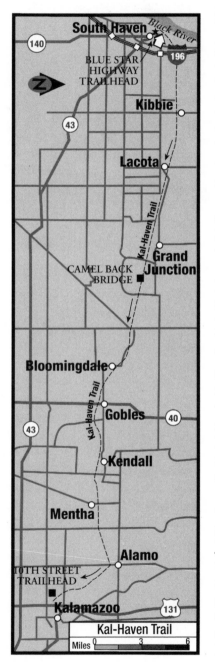

museum, with an accompanying caboose/information center. Gobles, just past the 20-mile mark, and Kendall, near mile 24, offer a variety of services, including food and camping. South of the trail at Mentha, at mile 25.5, is a large barn that was used to house horses and cattle back when this settlement was the world's largest producer of spearmint and peppermint.

At 33.5 miles, you will arrive at the eastern terminus of the Kal-Haven Trail, a restored train caboose located on 10th Street in Oshtemo Township near Kalamazoo. The city's distinctive name comes from an Indian phrase, Kee-Kalamazoo, meaning "where the water boils in the pot." The natives had discovered a number of bubbling springs in the river. For a time, the city went under the name Bronson, given to it by the first white settler in honor of himself, but the original name in its shortened form was again adopted in 1836.

Kalamazoo is well known for the cultivation of celery, which was introduced to the region in 1856 by James Taylor, a Scotsman who had imported celery seeds from England. By the 1870s, Dutch immigrants were draining nearby swamps and cultivating huge crops of celery. At about the same time, Dr. William E. Upjohn established

The shade-covered Kal-Haven Trail (photo by: Michael Sproul)

a small pill factory, which grew to become a cornerstone of the pharmaceutical industry.

RIDE GUIDE

- ★ 0.0 From the trailhead on Blue Star Highway in South Haven, ride east on the Kal-Haven Trail.
- 7.0 Lacota.
- 11.0 Camel Back Bridge.
- 15.9 Bloomingdale.
- 25.5 Mentha.
- 33.5 10th Street Trailhead. End of ride.

28 Coopersville Ramble
Submitted by A. G. Souter

This route leads through small towns west of Grand Rapids and through countryside that from late July through Labor Day is rich with plump, juicy blueberries. Watch for wildlife, especially deer.

Type of ride: road bike
Starting point: downtown Coopersville

Finishing point: same
Distance: 46.2 miles
Level of difficulty: moderate
General terrain: gentle terrain over alternately smooth and rough pavement
Traffic conditions: generally two-lane, with traffic ranging from nil to quite heavy; west of I-96, paved shoulders on the roads
Estimated riding time: 3 to 5 hours
Best season/time of day to ride: June through September
Points of interest: The all-volunteer Coopersville & Marne Railway Company offers excursions aboard a historic passenger train. Call (616) 837-7000 for a schedule and prices.
Accommodations and services: all services available along the loop, including a bike shop and campground in Grand Haven
Supplemental maps or other information: none

GETTING THERE
The ride begins at the public parking lot on the north side of downtown Coopersville. From west of Grand Rapids, exit I-96 into Coopersville, following the "Train" signs to downtown. There is plenty of parking available.

A slow Sunday morning in Coopersville (photo by: Arthur "Doc" Souter)

IN THE SADDLE

Leave the parking lot heading west and ride onto Ottawa Street, which curves northwesterly to pass the Northeast Ottawa District Library. In 0.2 mile, bear left (west) onto Spring Street. At 0.7 mile, at the end of Spring Street, turn right onto 64th Avenue. Here you can see the water tower and the offices and facilities of Leigh Products, a major manufacturer of ventilation equipment.

At 1.2 miles, turn left onto Cleveland Street. At 3.5 miles, State Road intersects with Cleveland; continue straight. At mile 6.6, cross Crockery Creek on a narrow bridge; then, at 6.9 miles, pass the entrance to the American Youth Soccer Organization. Enter Nunica at 7.1 miles. At 7.5 miles, cross Apple Drive and Main; then, at 7.7 miles, follow the sign reading "To West M104." Ride with particular caution where traffic merges from the right rear at 8.2 miles.

At 13.7 miles, Lake Street crosses M104 (now Savage Street), which has unusually high curbs in this area; stay far enough left to avoid clipping the curb with your pedal. At 15.1 miles, reach the apex of a bridge, from which you have a good view of Spring Lake to the north. Cross the Grand River at 15.4 miles. Use extra caution where Wilson Avenue crosses the route at 16.1 miles, as many cars make right-hand turns here to access the beach. Bear right here at the Y intersection onto 7th Street.

At 16.2 miles is the Rock 'n Road Bike Shop and also a Coast Guard motor lifeboat display. At 16.4 miles, turn right onto Washington and cross the railroad tracks. Washington ends at Harbor Street at mile 17.0, with the TriCity Historical Society on the right and the Chamber of Commerce on the left. Turn left toward Grand Haven State Park, entering the park in about a mile.

To begin the return trip via Eastmanville and Lamont, ride back along Harbor, crossing Washington Street at 18.7 miles. Stop and have a look at the static steam engine display at 18.9 miles; then, at 20.2 miles, re-cross the Grand River and bear right onto M104 (Savage Street). At mile 20.9, at the Arby's restaurant, turn south onto Cutler Street; then turn left onto Exchange Street at 21.0 miles. Pass the Spring Lake Post Office at 21.2 miles. At mile 21.9, where Exchange Street ends, turn right onto Lake Street. At 22.3 miles, turn left onto Leonard Street, following it across Lloyd's Bayou. Watch for deer!

At mile 31.9, turn right onto 104th Avenue; then turn left in 0.5 mile onto Oriole Drive. At mile 33.9, ride north (turn left) on 96th

Statue at the Ottawa County Courthouse (photo by: Arthur "Doc" Souter)

Avenue for 0.6 mile to an intersection and turn right onto Leonard Street. At mile 37.6, you will enter the community of Eastmanville, continuing on Leonard. Deer Creek Park, a day-use county park, is 0.5 mile south of the route at mile 39.8 (where 60th Avenue crosses Leonard Street). Continue on Leonard Street and enter the town of Lamont. Turn north onto 48th Avenue (Leonard continues as a boulevard).

At mile 44.4, turn left onto Randall Street (which is Arthur to the east). One mile farther, carefully cross the Coopersville & Marne Railway tracks, which are dangerously diagonal to the road. Continue on Randall. At mile 46, turn north onto Eastmanville Street (River Street goes south); then, at mile 46.2, re-cross the tracks adjacent to the train depot. You are back in downtown Coopersville.

RIDE GUIDE

★   0.0 From the public parking lot on the north side of
         Coopersville, ride west on Ottawa Street.
      0.2 Bear left onto Spring Street.
★   0.7 Turn right onto 64th Avenue.
★   1.2 Turn left onto Cleveland Street.
      7.1 Nunica.
      7.7 Follow "To West M104" sign.
     11.0 Blueberry Hill.
     15.1 Top of bridge.
     16.1 At **Y**, bear right onto Seventh Street.
★   16.4 Turn right onto Washington.
★   17.0 Turn left onto Harbor Street.

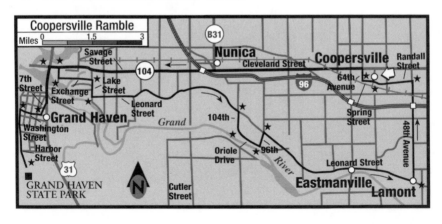

★ 17.8 Grand Haven State Park entrance. Turn around and retrace
    your route back to Washington Street.
★ 18.6 Turn right onto Washington Street.
★ 19.4 Turn left onto Seventh Street.
★ 19.7 Bear left onto US 31.
   20.2 Ride onto M104 (Savage Street).
★ 20.9 Turn south on Cutler Street.
★ 21.0 Turn left onto Exchange Street.
★ 21.9 Turn right onto Lake Street.
★ 22.3 Turn left onto Leonard Street.
   29.2 Cross Crockery Creek.
★ 31.9 Turn right onto 104th Avenue.
★ 32.4 Turn left onto Oriole Drive.
★ 33.2 Ride north on 96th Avenue.
★ 33.8 Turn right onto Leonard.
   37.6 Eastmanville.
   39.8 Cross Deer Creek.
   39.9 Lamont.
★ 40.8 Turn left onto 48th Avenue.
   43.9 Cross I-96.
★ 44.4 Turn left onto Randall Street.
★ 46.0 Turn right onto Eastmanville Street.
   46.2 End of ride.

Paw Paw Way
Submitted by Teri Simpson

Light traffic and gentle hills are the hallmarks of this route through the
fruit belt of southwestern Michigan. The route features vineyards and
cherry and apple orchards. There are beaches, golf, shops, and many
fine restaurants in Paw Paw and the surrounding area.

Type of ride: road bike
Starting point: Van Buren County Human Services building parking
   lot in Paw Paw
Finishing point: same

Distance: 34.8 miles

Level of difficulty: easy to moderate

General terrain: gentle hills

Traffic conditions: two-lane roads with some shoulders for riding and light to moderate traffic (lighter conditions before afternoon rush hour on weekdays)

Estimated riding time: 2 hours

Best season/time of day to ride: anytime except winter

Points of interest: fruit orchards, vineyards

Accommodations and services: beaches, golf, shops, and restaurants in and around Paw Paw

Supplemental maps or other information: a (helpful) Van Buren County map available from Michigan Department of Transportation, Highway Transportation Planning Services, P.O. Box 30050, Lansing, MI 48909

GETTING THERE

From I-94, take the Paw Paw exit into town on M40 North. Continue past St. Julian's Winery to the stoplight and turn left onto Michigan Avenue. Turn right at the second stoplight onto Hazen Street. Continue past the hospital to the parking lot at the Van Buren County Human Services building.

IN THE SADDLE

The town of Paw Paw took its name from the nearby river, which Native Americans named after the trees that grew along its shore. Paw Paw has long been the center of a booming vineyard region. Your ride will take you through several of these vineyards, as well as through blueberry fields.

From the starting point in the Human Services parking lot, turn left onto Hazen Street. It turns sharply to the left at mile 1.5, where the road becomes County Road 665. Turn right onto 44th Avenue, which leads into the countryside.

At 2.6 miles, turn right onto 35th Street and ride along blueberry orchards as your route turns into 46th Avenue after bending to the left. Stay on 46th until you cross M40 and come to 33rd Street. Turn left onto 33rd Street and follow the curve around to the right where the road

Faces on the barn (photo by: Jerry Petill)

becomes 45th Avenue. This road ends at County Road 653, at the 6-mile mark.

Turn right onto County Road 653, a fairly busy shortcut between Kalamazoo and Paw Paw. Continue south past small airstrips and roller coaster hills to the point where the route crosses M40 and becomes 32nd Street. From this point, the ride enters farmland and marsh country, which is prime land for growing blueberries.

The street dead-ends against County Road 358 at 12 miles. Turn left for a short side trip into Lawton, or turn right to continue the trip and see more farm country. County Road 358 also dead-ends, meeting Paw Paw Road at 16.6 miles. Turn right onto Paw Paw Road and after the cemetery turn left as Paw Paw Road continues. Paw Paw Road crosses M51 and heads into more orchard and fruit country, hay fields, and woods. The road ends at 46th Street, where the route goes to the right across rolling hills to Lake Cora.

At the bottom of a large hill at 22 miles, turn right onto Territorial Road. The railroad crossing on Territorial Road is very rough, so use caution and consider walking across. Stay on Territorial Road to Red

Arrow Highway. Follow Red Arrow Highway east to the Cora Lake Golf Course and County Road 671. Turn left on County Road 671 for a long climb through apple orchards to County Road 374.

Turn right onto County Road 374, which forms an S-curve past a cemetery as it slowly climbs to 41st Street at 25.6 miles. Turn left onto 41st Street and continue up to the "Top of the World" in the midst of a vineyard. Continue north to the bottom of the hill and turn right onto 52nd Avenue; then left (north) onto 40th Street. Turn right onto 47th Avenue at 27.6 miles and 2 miles later, turn right onto County Road 665. Remain on County Road 665 for the 5 curvy miles back to the Van Buren County Human Services building.

RIDE GUIDE

- ★   0.0 From the Van Buren County Human Services building, turn left onto Hazen Street.
-     1.5 The route changes to County Road 665.
- ★   1.7 Turn right onto 44th Avenue.
- ★   2.6 Turn right onto 35th Street. The route changes to 46th Avenue.
- ★   4.9 Turn left onto 33rd Street, which becomes 45th Avenue.
- ★   6.0 Turn right onto County Road 653.
-    10.5 The route becomes 32nd Street.

Michigan vineyards (photo by: Jerry Petill)

Take a dip in the Paw Paw River. (photo by: Jerry Petill)

★ 12.0 Turn right onto County Road 358.
★ 16.6 Turn right onto Paw Paw Road.
★ 17.0 Just past the cemetery, turn left to remain on Paw Paw Road.
17.8 Cross M51.
★ 19.3 Turn right onto 46th Street.
★ 21.4 Turn right onto Territorial Road, which joins Red Arrow Highway.
★ 22.9 Turn left onto County Road 671.
★ 24.0 Turn right onto County Road 374.
★ 25.6 Turn left onto 41st Street.
★ 24.6 Turn right onto 52nd Avenue.
★ 26.6 Turn left onto 40th Street.
★ 27.6 Turn right onto 47th Avenue.
★ 29.6 Turn right onto County Road 665.
34.7 Van Buren County Human Services building. End of ride.

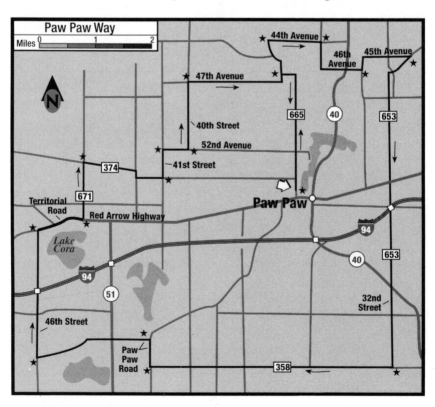

Holland-Saugatuck Connection
Submitted by Russ and Jane Dykstra

This very popular ride begins in the city of Holland, well known for the Dutch influences reflected in its architecture and cuisine—not to mention in the popularity and convenience of bicycling in the area. Saugatuck is a culturally diverse village that is a favorite destination for the region's artists, yachters, and beach goers. Gentle terrain and quiet, smooth roads make this a great outing for families with kids. There are plenty of places to eat and shop along the way.

Type of ride: road bike
Starting point: Centennial Park in downtown Holland, at the corner of 12th Street and River Avenue
Finishing point: downtown Saugatuck
Distance: 15 miles, one way
Level of difficulty: easy
General terrain: flat to gently rolling
Traffic conditions: light (except for a stretch on the Blue Star Highway, which has wide shoulders)

Buttersfield Park (photo by: Laurie James)

Be careful not to get burned. (photo by: Russ Dykstra)

Estimated riding time: 1 to 2 hours

Best season/time of day to ride: summer (plenty of shade) and fall; any time of any day (weekdays quieter)

Points of interest: great shopping and dining in Holland (2 blocks north of the starting point) and Saugatuck; Holland State Park and Saugatuck State Park (dunes)

Accommodations and services: all services available, including parking at both ends

Supplemental maps or other information: nice five-county map available from Universal Map, P.O. Box 15, 795 Progress Court, Williamston, MI 48895, (517) 655-5641

GETTING THERE
Holland is located approximately 25 miles southwest of Grand Rapids on I-196. Centennial Park is situated in downtown Holland at the corner of 12th Street and River Avenue.

IN THE SADDLE

From Centennial Park, head west down 12th Street to where it ends at 0.7 mile, at the shore of Lake Macatawa in beautiful Kollen Park. Bear left onto Kollen Park Drive, passing the boat ramp and the large Heinz pickle plant (nose-holding optional but recommended). Turn right onto 17th, following the bike path on the south side of the street. At 1.5 miles, 17th becomes South Shore Drive, which winds past gorgeous lakeside homes on its way to Lake Michigan.

At 5.1 miles, almost at the end of South Shore Drive, turn left onto 32nd Street, curving around the Eldean shipyard. At the next corner, turn right onto 66th Street, entering Allegan County. (Note: 32nd Street forms the line between Ottawa and Allegan Counties. The street numbering systems change when crossing that line: For example, 32nd Street in Holland is the same road as 148th Street in Allegan County.)

Follow this wide, shady, quiet street south for 4 miles, to 140th Street. (After about 2.5 miles, 66th Street curves around charming Gilligan Lake, a perfect place to stop and stretch.) Turn left onto 140th Street and, in 0.5 mile, turn right onto 65th Street. This road turns left to become Island Lake Road. Where Island Lake Road dead-ends, turn right onto 64th Street. In a mile, at a cumulative mileage of 12.5, turn right onto the wide shoulder of the potentially busy Blue Star Highway. (You can cut through the restaurant's parking lot, thereby avoiding the busy 64th Street–Blue Star intersection.)

In a mile, turn right at the second Saugatuck sign, at the corner of 134th and Blue Star Highway. 134th becomes North Street and winds down and up before running into Holland Street. Turn left onto Holland Street, watching both ways for traffic. At the bottom of the hill, at 14.6 miles, is the picturesque Peterson Mill, one of countless attractions in this unique town. Continue along the Kalamazoo River, which leads you to downtown Saugatuck before it empties into Lake Michigan.

The boat- and people-watching along Saugatuck's waterfront can't be beat. One possible activity is the Saugatuck Chain Ferry, which will take you on a short, human-powered trip across the Kalamazoo River. From the opposite bank, it is a short but hilly ride to the outstanding Oval Beach on Lake Michigan. The best way back to Holland is to backtrack and see the opposite side of everything you encountered on the way to Saugatuck.

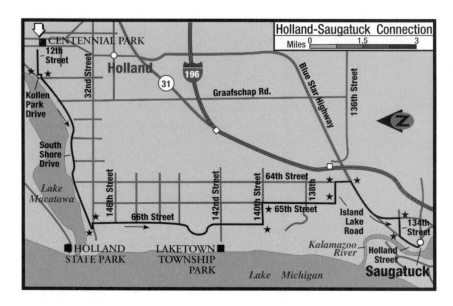

RIDE GUIDE

   0.0 From Centennial Park in Holland, ride west onto 12th
         Street.
★ 1.1 Turn left onto Kollen Park Drive.
★ 1.3 Turn right onto 17th Street.
   1.5 Ride onto South Shore Drive.
★ 5.1 Turn left onto 32nd Street.
★ 5.2 Turn right onto 66th Street.
★ 8.7 Turn left onto 140th Street.
★ 9.4 Turn right onto 65th Street.
★ 11.2 Turn left onto Island Lake Road.
★ 11.5 Turn right onto 64th Street.
★ 11.7 Turn right onto Blue Star Highway.
★ 12.6 Turn right onto 134th Street.
★ 13.7 Turn left onto Holland Street.
  14.6 Peterson Mill.
  15.0 Oval Beach. End of ride.

Region 4:
Southeast Michigan

Bridge between Half Moon and Watson Lake (photo by: Carol Otto)

Pinckney Dirt Ride
31
Submitted by Carol Otto

Ride around Half Moon Lake north of Ann Arbor for a series of scenic outlooks, wooden bridges, and several challenging hills.

Type of ride: mountain bike
Starting point: Pinckney State Recreation Area
Finishing point: same
Distance: 1.9 miles (Silver Lake), 5.1 miles (Crooked Lake), 17.5 miles (Potawatomi)
Level of difficulty: moderate (Silver Lake) and hard (Crooked Lake, Potawatomi)
General terrain: dirt, gravel, and sand two-track roads, with several tough hills
Traffic conditions: no mechanized vehicles, but all routes shared with hikers
Estimated riding time: 0.5 to 2.5 hours
Best season/time of day to ride: weekdays, late spring through fall
Points of interest: dense forests, scenic overlooks
Accommodations and services: all services available in the village of Pinckney, including campgrounds, groceries, restaurants, and bike service
Supplemental maps or other information: Pinckney State Recreation Area, 8555 Silver Hill, Route 1, Pinckney, MI 48169, (313) 426-4913

GETTING THERE
From Ann Arbor, follow US 23 north to North Territorial Road (exit 49). Go 10 miles west to Dexter-Townhall Road and turn right. At Silver Hill Road, turn left into the Pinckney State Recreation Area. The trailhead is located at the south edge of the parking area.

IN THE SADDLE
From the trailhead, ride up two challenging dirt hills to the Potawatomi and Silver Lake Trails. These two trails share the same path for 0.5 mile before dividing. Watch for wooden signs to mark the location where they diverge. The Silver Lake Trail extends another mile to reach the Crooked Lake Trail. Of these three trails, the

Silver Lake Picnic and Recreation Area (photo by: Carol Otto)

Potawatomi is marked with mileposts while the other two are not.

The Potawatomi, known as the "Pota" by local cyclists, is the most challenging of the three trails and is the one described here and in the Ride Guide. It extends past Pickerel Lake at Marker 31.5, Crooked Lake at Marker 38, Gosling Lake at Marker 41, and Blind Lake and Half Moon Lake at Marker 46. The trail includes several scenic overlooks in the midst of heavily wooded terrain and wooden bridges crossing lowland areas.

There is a very challenging hill at Marker 30, as well as very steep slopes to the left of the trail between Markers 29 and 31. A sand pit also presents a challenge at Marker 45. There is an option to cut several miles off the route by way of a marked shortcut immediately following the sand pit.

RIDE GUIDE

    0.0 From the parking lot, ride to the trailhead at the south edge of the lot.

★ 0.6 Turn left onto Potawatomi Trail.

4.1 Bear left to continue on Potawatomi Trail.

★ 4.9 Turn right onto Hankerd Road.

★ 5.1 Turn left onto Potawatomi Trail.

6.8 Marker 29. Bear right to continue on Potawatomi Trail.

8.6 Marker 45.

9.4 Bear left to continue on Potawatomi Trail.

9.8 Cross Patterson Lake Road.

10.6 Cross Doyle Road.

11.3 Cross Doyle Road again.

13.0 Cross Patterson Lake Road again.

★ 15.0 Bear left to continue on Potawatomi Trail.

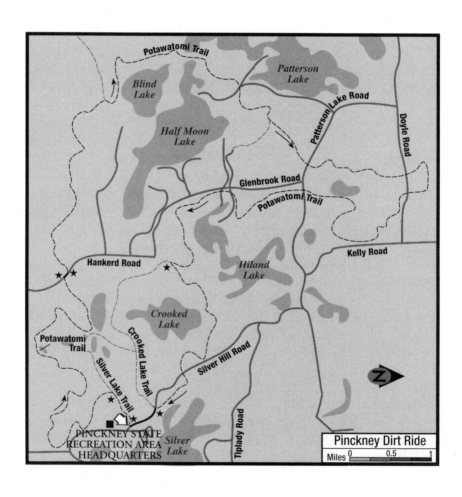

A unique spot to explore (photo by: Carol Otto)

16.6 Bear left to continue on Potawatomi Trail.
★ 16.9 Turn left onto Silver Hill Road.
★ 17.3 Turn left toward parking lot.
17.5 Parking lot. End of ride.

32 Ann Arbor Century
Submitted by Lew Kidder

This ride will take you on a loop through farm and resort areas of southeast Michigan, including a short stretch along the Huron River. You will also pass by several lakes and swimming beaches.

Type of ride: road bike
Starting point: Barton Park in Ann Arbor
Finishing point: same
Distance: 102.4 miles
Level of difficulty: moderate
General terrain: alternating hilly and flat
Traffic conditions: bike-friendly roads
Estimated riding time: 6 to 10 hours, depending on your speed and number of stops
Best season/time of day to ride: May through October

Points of interest: Paint Creek Trail; Dexter Cider Mill
Accommodations and services: all services available at towns and parks
   along the way
Supplemental maps or other information: Detroit and Southeast
   Michigan map available from AAA

GETTING THERE

Follow Main Street north from downtown Ann Arbor. Turn left on
Huron River Drive and follow it under the M14 expressway and down
a hill. Barton Park is about a mile farther on the right side of the road.
It is a city-owned park, and parking is free.

If you are approaching Ann Arbor from the north or east, follow
the M14 expressway south and west from US 23 and take the Main
Street exit. Huron River Drive is on the right about 200 yards after passing underneath M14.

IN THE SADDLE

Ann Arbor, home to the University of Michigan, is the trading center
of a large agricultural and fruit-producing region. There are two stories as to how the community came by its name, each with its staunch
proponents. The first story relates how, in the early 1820s, two couples
settled on what is today Allens Creek; both of the wives shared the first
name of Ann. Together, they built an arbor to train wild grapevines.
When a name for the settlement was chosen, the townspeople paid hom-
age to the first settlers by calling it Anns' Arbor, which was shortened
to its present form. The other account concerns a woman who guided
settlement parties out of Detroit as early as 1813. Her name was Ann
d'Arbeur. She later settled on a hillside above the Huron River and continued to guide settlers beyond that point. The town was named in her
honor, but the spelling was simplified. Take your pick of stories.

From Barton Park in Ann Arbor, turn right on Huron River Drive
and follow it upstream along the river. Cross the river at about 3 miles
and after an additional 0.75 mile pass Delhi Metropark on the left. Depending on the time of year, there may be anglers, kayakers, swimmers,
and other folks enjoying the water.

At 6.9 miles is the entrance to Dexter-Huron Metropark, where
water, restrooms, and picnic tables are found. These features are
common to all the parks along this route. Turn left on Mast Road at

the 8-mile mark and look across the river for the Dexter Cider Mill, established in 1886. It offers fresh-pressed cider and fry cakes in season. Continue across the railroad tracks where Mast Road becomes Central as it enters the village of Dexter.

Continue through Dexter on Main Street and across Warrior Creek, where the road name changes again to Dexter-Pinckney Road. At 9.1 miles, there is a traffic light and one more name change; the road now becomes Island Lake Road. Continue straight ahead to Dexter-Townhall Road at 11.8 miles, turn right, and follow Dexter-Townhall Road to the junction with North Territorial at 14.7 miles. Turn left onto North Territorial and follow it to the junction with Hankerd Road at 16.2 miles. Turn right onto Hankerd Road.

This section of the trip traverses the glacial lake region of southeast Michigan. In addition to forming most of the lakes, the glaciers also left many short, steep hills. At 18.3 miles, Hankerd Road changes to Glenbrook. Continue on to the intersection at 19.9 miles and turn left onto Patterson Lake Road. The route crosses the Potawatomi Trail, an extensive series of single-track bike and hiking trails developed on state land (see Ride 31, Pinckney Dirt Ride). They are quite difficult and require a mountain bike.

Continue for another 5 miles to the stop sign at M106 in the village of Gregory. Turn right onto M106, and follow it across the Lakeland Trails State Park, until it merges with M36. In another 0.5 mile, turn left on Dexter Trail and follow it to Main Street in Stockbridge, at the 30.3-mile mark. The actual village is another mile farther. Ride west from the town square on M52 for 0.5 mile, where the road splits. Continue straight on Morton Road. Turn left onto Heeney, which takes you past many farms that have been owned by the same families for more than one hundred years.

Turn left onto Parman at 36.1 miles, right onto Fitchburg at 36.9 miles, left onto Freiermuth at 37.9 miles, and left onto Base Line Road at 38.9 miles. A short distance later, the blacktop turns to the right and becomes Fitchburg Road. Turn left onto North Territorial and right onto Musback, which takes you through a working dairy farm and eventually to Plum Orchard Road/M106. Crossing Plum Orchard, Musback changes into Coonhill Road, and you enter the village of Munith. Continue out of Munith on Coonhill Road; then ride back into lake country by turning left onto Portage Lake Road.

At 48.1 miles, turn right onto Seymour Road. Follow it for 2 miles and then turn left onto Race Road, where the road is hilly and the surroundings are heavily forested. After passing under I-94, turn right onto Ann Arbor Road and then left onto Portage Road through the town of Leoni. Past Leoni, turn left on Napoleon Road and ride through Michigan's great watershed divide.

After crossing M60, turn left onto Stony Lake Road, which crosses M60 again and enters the village of Napoleon. Turn left onto East Street, right onto Cady, and then left again onto Wolf Lake Road. At 70.8 miles, turn right onto Michigan Avenue and ride into the village of Grass Lake. Turn right onto South Union Street, which bends left and becomes Grass Lake Road as it leaves the village. Turn left onto Francisco Road, which becomes Clear Lake Road as it crosses I-94. Turn right onto Harvey Road and continue past Pond Lily Lake. This is a migration stop for sand hill cranes, which are abundant around dusk in late October through early November.

At 80.7 miles, Harvey Road changes to Cavanaugh Lake Road; 5 miles later, you will round a sharp right and then bear left into the village of Chelsea. Chelsea is home to actor Jeff Daniels' Purple Rose Theater. Continue east through Chelsea, turn left onto McKinley Street, cross the railroad tracks, and turn right onto Railroad Street. This leads out of the village and becomes Dexter-Chelsea Road.

At the T intersection, turn right and follow the small hill into Dexter. Follow the road to the left onto Central Street, keeping the bandstand to your right. Central Street leads around and down, across the Huron River, and back to Huron River Drive. Turn right and, in the last 8 miles, retrace the first part of your route back to Barton Park in Ann Arbor.

RIDE GUIDE

★ 0.0 From Barton Park in Ann Arbor, turn right onto Huron River Drive.

3.1 Cross the Huron River.

3.8 Cross the Huron River again.

★ 8.0 Turn left onto Mast.

8.2 The route becomes Central Street.

8.5 The route becomes Main Street.

8.8 The route becomes Dexter-Pinckney Road.

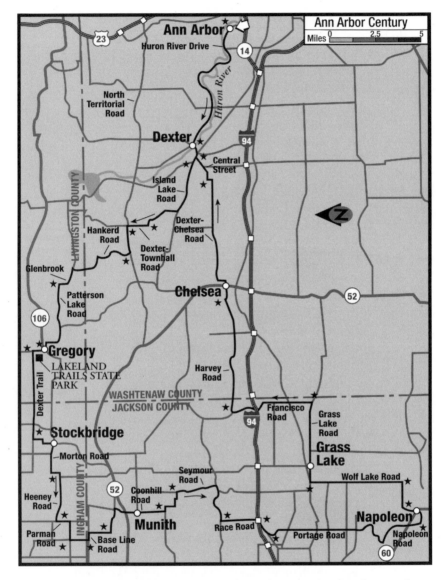

9.1 Ride through the traffic light and onto Island Lake Road.
★ 11.8 Turn right onto Dexter-Townhall Road.
★ 14.7 Turn left onto North Territorial Road.
★ 16.2 Turn right onto Hankerd Road.
18.3 The route changes names to Glenbrook.

★ 19.9 At the T intersection, turn left onto Patterson Lake Road.

20.0 Cross Potawatomi Trail.

21.0 The route changes names to Doyle.

★ 25.0 Turn right onto M106.

★ 25.6 Turn left onto Dexter Trail.

★ 30.3 Turn left onto Main Street.

31.6 Stockbridge.

32.1 Ride straight onto Morton Road.

★ 33.1 Turn left onto Heeney.

★ 36.1 Turn left onto Parman.

★ 36.9 Turn right onto Fitchburg.

★ 37.9 Turn left onto Freiermuth.

★ 38.9 Turn left onto Base Line Road.

39.2 The route changes names to Fitchburg Road.

★ 40.4 Turn left onto North Territorial.

42.4 The route changes names to Coonhill Road.

★ 43.1 Turn left onto Portage Lake Road.

★ 48.1 Turn right onto Seymour Road.

★ 50.1 Turn left onto Race Road.

★ 52.4 Turn right onto Ann Arbor Road.

★ 53.2 Turn left onto Portage Road.

★ 60.0 Turn left onto Napoleon Road.

★ 62.6 Turn left onto Stony Lake Road.

★ 63.4 Turn left onto East Street.

★ 64.4 At the T intersection, turn right onto Cady.

★ 65.6 Turn left onto Wolf Lake Road.

★ 70.8 At the T intersection, turn right onto Michigan Avenue.

★ 71.6 Turn right onto South Union Street.

72.0 The route becomes Grass Lake Road.

★ 75.1 Turn left onto Francisco Road.

78.7 The route becomes Clear Lake Road.

★ 79.7 Turn right onto Harvey Road.

80.7 The route changes names to Cavanaugh Lake Road.

★ 85.7 Cross railroad tracks and turn left onto Middle Street.

★ 86.8 Turn left onto McKinley Street.

87.4 The route becomes Dexter-Chelsea Road.

★ 93.7 At the T intersection, turn right onto Dexter.

★ 93.9 Bear left onto Central Street.

★ 94.4 Turn right onto Huron River Drive.
★ 102.4 Barton Park. End of ride.

Paint Creek Trail
Submitted by Alexander B. McGarry

This short ride along a rail-trail conversion project leads to two villages and other attractions, including a cider mill. The grades are gentle, offering plenty of opportunities to see the sights. The Paint Creek Trail makes a great outing for families on bikes.

Type of ride: mountain bike
Starting point: Rochester Municipal Parking Lot
Finishing point: same
Distance: 8.4 miles, one way
Level of difficulty: easy/moderate
General terrain: gentle upgrades on gravel trails

The Paint Creek cider mill—a nice spot for a rest (photo by: Alexander McGarry)

The first bridge on the trail (photo by: Alexander McGarry)

Traffic conditions: light
Estimated riding time: 1 hour
Best season/time of day to ride: fall mornings
Points of interest: wildlife (primarily deer), an apple cider mill, a trout stream, and wildflowers in season
Accommodations and services: full services available in Rochester; trail patrolled by Oakland County bike and horse patrols
Supplemental maps or other information: Paint Creek Trailway Commission, 4393 Collins Road, Rochester, MI 48306, (810) 651-9260

GETTING THERE
In Rochester, just north of metropolitan Detroit, turn onto Pine Street from University Avenue and travel one block north to the municipal parking lot next to Rochester City Hall.

IN THE SADDLE
Begin the trail at the Rochester Municipal Park, which straddles Paint Creek. Just north of the Ludlow Street crossing in the park is

the Dinosaur Hill Nature Preserve, with a woodchipped trail leading through thick forests alongside Paint Creek.

Head north across Tienken Road and Dutton Road. At Gallagher Road, turn right and follow the road to the Paint Creek Cider Mill. Leaving the mill, head north up the long grade to the Adams Road crossing. Watch for deer on the trail in this area, especially at sunrise and sunset. After the crossing, be sure to stay on the trail where it runs parallel to the Royal Oak Archery Club range.

The route passes through a tree-shaded area finally reaching the village of Lake Orion. The trail ends abruptly at a strip mall parking lot. The return trip retraces the trail back to the starting point.

RIDE GUIDE

0.0 From the Rochester Municipal Park, ride onto the Paint Creek Trail.

0.8 Cross Tienken Road.

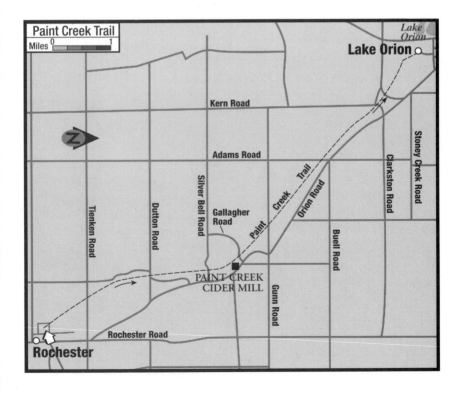

2.0 Cross Dutton Road.
3.0 Cross Silver Bell Road.
3.6 Cross Gallagher Road.
4.4 Cross Gunn Road.
5.8 Cross Adams Road.
7.3 Cross Kern and Clarkston Roads.
8.4 Lake Orion area. End of ride.

Tip of the Thumb Run
Submitted by Robert Weishaupt

This loop route follows the tip of the peninsula that makes up the thumb of Michigan's mitten-shaped landmass.

Type of ride: road bike
Starting point: Unionville-Sebewaing High School
Finishing point: same

Sanilac petroglyphs (photo by: Robert Weishaupt)

Distance: 132 miles
Level of difficulty: difficult
General terrain: flat to gently rolling
Traffic conditions: mostly light, with heavier traffic during the boating season
Estimated riding time: 2 days
Best season/time of day to ride: late spring through early fall
Points of interest: Pre-Columbian petroglyphs; world's largest human-made harbor
Accommodations and services: several hotels, motels, and a bed-and-breakfast available at Harbor Beach
Supplemental maps or other information: Harbor Beach hotel and motel information available at (517) 479-3645

GETTING THERE
Take the M25 exit from I-75 to the Unionville-Sebewaing High School, located between the two towns. You will need permission to park overnight in the school lot.

IN THE SADDLE
Ride south from the school on M25 approximately 3 miles to Unionville. Turn left on Cass Street, which becomes Bay City–Forestville Road. At 26 miles, turn left for a 2-mile side trip to the Sanilac pre-Columbian sandstone petroglyphs. Return to the main road and continue east to Forestville.

At 48 miles, turn left on M25 and follow it to Harbor Beach. Traffic along M25 should be light for this part of the trip. Downtown Harbor Beach is at 61 miles and includes several museums and the world's largest human-made harbor. This is near the halfway point of the ride and makes a good place to spend the night.

On the second day, continue north on M25. The road does not have a paved shoulder between Harbor Beach and Port Hope, but the traffic is usually light. At 76 miles, turn right onto Lighthouse Road to Pointe Aux Barques Lighthouse County Park. Three miles after the park, ride straight onto Pioneer Drive and pass through the village of Huron City. The route rejoins M25 at mile 81.

Follow M25 for 2 miles; then turn right onto Pearson Road. Where Pearson Road becomes Spring Street, continue to Grindstone

Pointe Aux Barques Lighthouse (photo by: Robert Weishaupt)

City and Port Austin. Rejoin M25 again at 90 miles, and follow it past the sand dunes and beaches of Port Crescent State Park and Albert Sleeper State Park.

One mile after the paved shoulder ends, turn right onto Weale Road; then turn left onto Kunl, right onto Geiger, left onto Riole, right onto Haist, and left onto Rose Island Road. Follow Rose Island into Sebewaing, where M25 joins the route one last time to lead south for the 3 miles back to your starting point.

RIDE GUIDE

   0.0 From the high school parking lot outside of Unionville, ride
       south on M25.
★ 3.3 Turn left (east) onto Cass Street, which becomes Bay City–
       Forestville Road.
★ 48.1 Forestville. Turn left onto M25.
  61.1 Harbor Beach.
★ 76.2 Turn right onto Lighthouse Road.
★ 80.2 Ride straight onto Pioneer Drive.
★ 81.1 Turn right onto M25.
★ 83.2 Turn right onto Pearson Road.
  84.1 Grindstone City.
★ 90.2 Turn right onto M25.
  96.1 Port Crescent State Park.

Keep your wheels to the Grindstone (photo by: Robert Weishaupt)

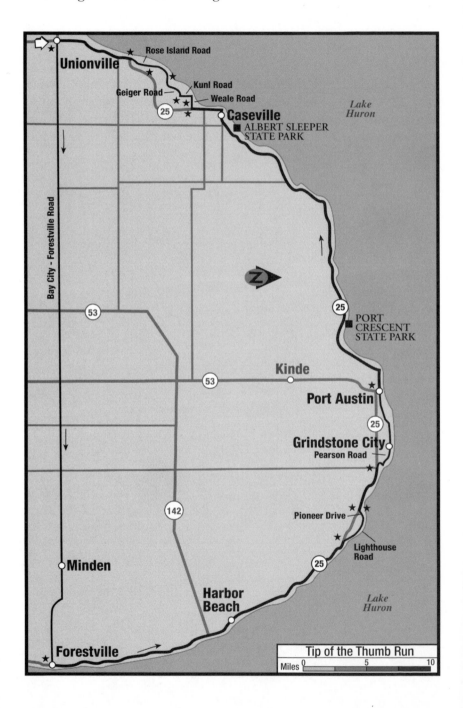

Unionville

Rose Island Road

Geiger Road

Kunl Road

Weale Road

25

Caseville

■ ALBERT SLEEPER
STATE PARK

Lake
Huron

Bay City - Forestville Road

53

25

PORT
CRESCENT
STATE PARK

Kinde

53

Port Austin

25

Grindstone City

Pearson Road

142

Pioneer Drive

Lighthouse
Road

25

Minden

Harbor
Beach

Lake
Huron

Forestville

Tip of the Thumb Run

Miles 0   5   10

★ 122.0 Turn right onto Weale Road.
★ 123.0 Turn left onto Kunl.
★ 124.3 Turn right onto Geiger.
★ 124.8 Turn left onto Ridge Street.
★ 125.5 Turn right onto Haist.
★ 126.1 Turn left onto Rose Island Road.
★ 129.3 Turn right onto M25.
    132.0 High school parking lot. End of ride.

Bald Mountain Trail
Submitted by Joy and Aribert Neumann

This collection of trails in the Bald Mountain Recreation Area, north of Detroit, offers a variety of off-road experiences.

Type of ride: mountain bike
Starting point: Bald Mountain Recreation Area
Finishing point: same
Distance: varies
Level of difficulty: moderate
General terrain: smooth and level on improved trails; sand, bogs, and minor hazards on unimproved sections
Traffic conditions: off-road trails, no traffic
Estimated riding time: 1 to 2 hours
Best season/time of day to ride: April through October
Points of interest: Bald Mountain State Recreation Area
Accommodations and services: none within the park
Supplemental maps or other information: North Oakland County maps available from local bookstores and Kmart; Bald Mountain Recreation Area trail maps available from the park headquarters at 1330 Greenshield Road, Route 1, Lake Orion, MI 48360, (810) 693-6767

GETTING THERE
From the Detroit area, drive north on I-75 to the junction with M24. Turn right (north) onto M24 and follow it to the junction with Creek

Road. Turn right onto Creek Road and follow it for 2 miles to the junction with Adams Road. Turn left onto Adams Road and follow it until it ends. Turn right onto Stoney Road, and then take a quick left onto Harmon Road. This road will take you into the park. At the junction with Predmore Road, turn right onto Predmore and follow it for just under 1 mile to the parking lot at the trailhead, which will be on your left.

A state park motor vehicle permit is required to drive into the Bald Mountain Recreation Area, as well as other state parks in Michigan. The permits are $4 per day, or $20 for a yearly pass that will admit you to all state parks.

IN THE SADDLE

This mountain bike loop tour will take you through the Bald Mountain Recreation Area, a 4,600-acre park open seven days a week. This is good off-road riding, but be prepared to get dirty, especially in the spring. The terrain consists of some bogs, sand, mud, tree roots, and, at times, standing water. Most sections of the trails are in excellent shape for fun riding, and trail maintenance by the park staff is very good.

In summer, especially after a rainy spring, in some sections you may find yourself swooshing through tall grass up to your elbows. In these conditions, insect repellent is a must.

There are many variations on the basic loop within the park. Just watch the map, and compare it to the trail signs if you want a shorter or longer variation. Note that in the past the trails have been identified by a color scheme (Orange Trail, Blue Trail, and so on). Park personnel are in the process of converting the color system to a numbering system. The map in this book uses the newer system, but if you have an older map of the recreation area, it may show the color system.

The Bald Mountain Recreation Area was established in 1946, when many areas in southeast Michigan were designated as recreation parks. The trails were originally designed primarily for cross-country skiing, but in the summer the trails are now open for hiking and bicycling. In the winter, the trails in the southern portion of the park can also be used for snowmobiling when there is more than four inches of snow. (If you get to Bald Mountain in the winter, it has one of the best sledding hills in northern Oakland County.)

The Recreation Area has recently implemented a wet-weather policy for the trails. When the trails get muddy enough that substantial damage could be caused by bikes, they are closed. If you are planning to ride during a wet time of year, you might want to call ahead and check on the trail conditions. Generally, the park personnel discourage mountain bike riding between early March and early April, during the time of spring thaw. However, if there is a freeze at that time (which is not uncommon, particularly in March) the trails will be opened for riding. The same riding limitations may occur in the fall. The trails are well-drained, and it would take an unusually heavy amount of rainfall to cause them to be closed during the summer.

The suggested large loop ride begins at the trailhead, just off Predmore Road. Start at Trail Marker 17. At the junction with Marker 16, make a left turn, and follow the loop in a clockwise direction.

There are no services within the park, other than occasional pit toilets (at least one located on each loop). A toilet is located at the start of the ride near the junction of Markers 16 and 17. There is a toilet and water pump between Markers 2 and 3; there also are some rustic cabins in this area that may be rented (inquire at the park office).

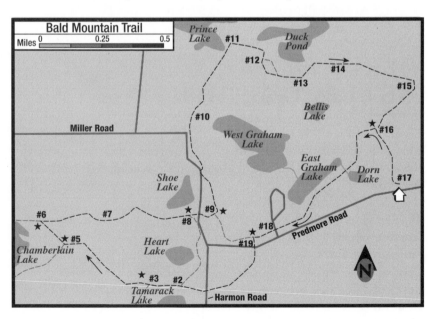

Along with other cyclists and hikers, you most likely will be sharing the trails with deer and other wildlife. Keep your speeds down so everyone can enjoy the trails.

The park office, in the southern portion of the park, is located on the original site of the area's first township hall, which also served as the region's first post office. Park personnel are trying to get the building and grounds designated as an official historic site.

RIDE GUIDE

    0.0 From the the trailhead off Predmore Road, ride north from the #17 trail marker

★   0.3 At #16 trail marker, turn left.

★   1.0 At #19 trail marker, turn left.

    1.8 At #2 trail marker, continue straight.

★   2.0 At #3 trail marker, bear to the right.

★   2.3 At #5 trail marker, bear to the right.

★   2.5 At #6 trail marker, turn right.

★   3.2 At #8 trail marker, bear to the left.

★   3.3 At #9 trail marker, bear to the left.

★   5.5 At #16 trail marker, bear to the left.

    5.8 #17 trail marker. End of ride.

36 Lake Orion Trail
Submitted by Joy and Aribert Neumann

This ride, of moderate difficulty, follows part of a rail-trail and takes you to Lake Orion and the Bald Mountain Recreation Area, just north of Detroit.

Type of ride: road bike
Starting point: Stony Creek Metro Park
Finishing point: same
Distance: 23.9 miles
Level of difficulty: moderate
General terrain: flat to gently rolling
Traffic conditions: mostly light, with some heavier traffic in the

Lake Orion area
Estimated riding time: 3 to 4 hours
Best season/time of day to ride: April to October
Points of interest: Paint Creek Trail, Lake Orion, and Bald Mountain
State Recreation Area
Accommodations and services: all services available in northern Detroit suburbs; groceries and restaurants available in Lake Orion
Supplemental maps or other information: none

GETTING THERE
From M53 (north out of Detroit), take the 26-Mile Road exit west to Stony Creek Metro Park. The park entrance fee is $3. Park at the West Branch Picnic Area A1B.

IN THE SADDLE
From the West Branch Picnic Area, turn left onto Stony Creek Park Road. At 0.4 mile turn left onto the first service road and ride around the gate. Follow this gravel road to the end and bear right through another pedestrian gate.

At 1.2 miles, turn left onto Snell Road. At 3.6 miles, turn right onto Orion Road. Just past the Paint Creek Cider Mill, turn left onto Gallagher Road at 3.8 miles. At 3.9 miles, turn right again at the creek and onto the Paint Creek Trail, a converted rail-trail. From here, you can turn south to get to the Rochester Municipal Park and nearby Rochester, with food and accommodations available. As the ride continues, you will head to the northwest, paralleling Orion Road, toward the community of Lake Orion.

You will find many places to stop and linger along the Paint Creek Trail. Along this section of the trail, there are several good spots for wading if it is a hot day and many good places to spot birds and wildlife.

At mile 9.3, the Paint Creek Trail ends behind a grocery store and restaurant in Lake Orion. If you prefer outdoor eating, you can pick up groceries and go to the Perry City Park. From the end of the Paint Creek Trail, go one block left to Atwater; turn left onto Atwater. Then turn left onto Perry Road. The city park, with restrooms available, is on the left.

To depart Lake Orion, at mile 9.8 turn right onto Flint and then left onto Miller Road. There can be high traffic in this area, so use

Victorian manor in Rochester (photo by: Aribert Neumann)

caution. At the intersection with Conklin Road (mile 10.4), turn right onto Conklin (there is a convenience store just to the left).

In another 0.2 mile, you can turn left and enter the Bald Mountain Recreation Area for some great single-track trails, assuming you brought your mountain bike and are up for some off-road riding (see Ride 35, Bald Mountain Trail). Watch for the trailhead across from Ferguson Street and next to a mailbox with the number 160 on it. There are no other trailhead indications. Watch for maps mounted on posts.

To continue the Lake Orion ride, remain on Miller Road and, at the intersection with Stony Creek Park Road, turn left. At 13.5 miles, turn left onto Lake George Road; 0.5 mile later, turn right onto Predmore Road at the T intersection. Follow Predmore Road through a ninety-degree turn to the south, where it is joined by Kline Road. You will cross Rochester Road at 16.7 miles.

At the intersection of Predmore Road and Rush Road (17.6 miles), turn right onto Rush Road. This road sign is often missing, so expect it to be gone. At 18.7 miles, your route curves left onto Parks Road, and at 19.7 miles, you will turn right onto Dequindre Road.

At 21 miles, bear right onto Mount Vernon Road; at 22.5 miles, ride through the pedestrian gate straight onto Stony Creek Park Road. Stay on Stony Creek Park Road for 1 mile, and then turn right into the West Branch Picnic Area.

RIDE GUIDE

★   0.0 From the West Branch Picnic Area parking lot at Stony Creek Metro Park, ride back to Stony Creek Park Road and turn left.

★   0.4 Turn left onto the first service road and ride around the gate. Follow the gravel road to the end and bear right.

★   1.2 Turn left onto Snell Road.

★   3.6 Turn right onto Orion Road.

★   3.8 Turn left onto Gallagher Road.

★   3.9 Turn right onto Paint Creek Trail.

7.8 Cross Clarkston Road.

★   9.3 Turn right onto Atwater.

★   9.5 Turn left onto Perry Road.

★   9.8 Turn right onto Flint.

★   9.9 Turn left onto Miller Road.

★   10.4 Turn right onto Conklin Road.
★   10.7 Turn left onto the single-track trail, across from Ferguson Street, and ride into the Bald Mountain Recreation Area.
★   11.1 Turn left onto Stony Creek Park Road.
★   13.5 Turn left onto Lake George Road.
★   14.0 Turn right onto Predmore Road.
      16.7 Cross Rochester Road.
★   17.6 Turn right onto Rush Road.
★   18.7 Bear left onto Parks Road.
★   19.7 Turn right onto Dequindre Road.
      21.0 Bear right onto Mount Vernon Road.
★   22.5 Turn right onto Snell Road.
★   22.7 Turn left onto gravel road; then bear left and follow to Parks Road.
★   23.5 Turn right onto Parks Road.
★   23.9 Turn right into the West Branch Picnic Area. End of ride.

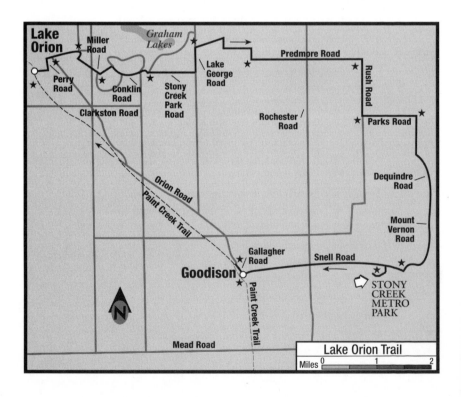

Dexter Ramble
Submitted by Ken and Viki Shayna

On this ride, you will travel through farmland to the lakes region, including the Waterloo State Recreation Area. This route serves as a hub for numerous side trips that depart from it, including rides to two state recreation areas.

Type of ride: road bike
Starting point: Dexter
Finishing point: same
Distance: 41.7 miles
Level of difficulty: moderate
General terrain: two-lane country roads, some hilly sections
Traffic conditions: moderate traffic on short stretches, but very light traffic for the balance
Estimated riding time: 2 hours
Best season/time of day to ride: April through October
Points of interest: lakes, farm country
Accommodations and services: full services available at the beginning of the route, and other facilities available in villages along the way
Supplemental maps or other information: none

GETTING THERE
Take I-94 to the Baker Road exit; then go 3 miles north into downtown Dexter. The ride begins by the Dexter Clock at the intersection of Dexter–Ann Arbor Road and Broad Street.

IN THE SADDLE
Dexter was named after Judge Samuel W. Dexter, who built a large Greek Revival–style house here in 1841. You begin riding from the Dexter Clock in the downtown area. Head west past the A&W restaurant to the stoplight across from Burton Hall. The road forks, and most traffic moves to the right toward Pinckney. Follow the road straight ahead up a moderate hill on Island Lake Road.

The next 3 miles pass a mix of agriculture land and housing subdivisions. There are steep and long moderate hills on this road, made more difficult by prevailing northwest winds.

Turn right at the red barn onto Dexter-Townhall Road, and follow it north approximately 3 miles to North Territorial Road. Turn left (west) onto North Territorial, a former stagecoach route between Detroit and Chicago, which is heavily traveled. Turn right onto Hankerd Road and travel north into the lakes country. This part of the route is marked by many steep hills and winding roads. There are ample opportunities for side trips to the many lakes along this road.

Just past the sign marking the Livingston County limits is a channel connecting Half Moon Lake and Hiland Lake. The inhabitants of the house on the northwest corner of the bridge (11860 Hankerd) have placed a water line near the road for cyclist use (Thanks!). Continue north and turn left onto Patterson Lake Road; then left again onto Doyle Road. Ride through a forested area and open corn fields; then turn left onto Unadilla Road.

The Unadilla Store is down the road about a mile, followed by a sharp left and right in the road. Past Wild Goose Lake and North Lake, the road makes a steep climb back to North Territorial Road. Continue south, and the road now becomes Stofer. The scenery is a mixture of newer homes and farms. Take a right onto Island Lake Road followed by a left onto Werkner Road. This road ends at M52 (Stockbridge-

The clock tower in downtown Dexter (photo by: Ken Shayna)

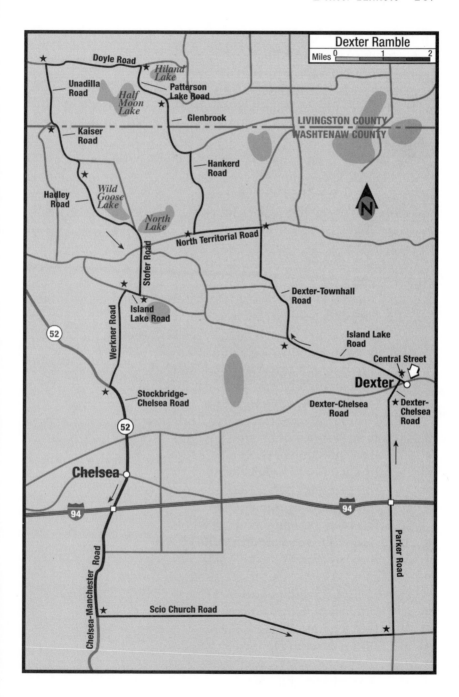

Dexter Ramble

Miles 0   1   2

Doyle Road

Hiland Lake

Patterson Lake Road

Unadilla Road

Half Moon Lake

Glenbrook

LIVINGSTON COUNTY
WASHTENAW COUNTY

Kaiser Road

Hankerd Road

Hadley Road

Wild Goose Lake

North Lake

North Territorial Road

Stofer Road

Dexter-Townhall Road

Island Lake Road

Island Lake Road

Central Street

Werkner Road

52

Stockbridge-Chelsea Road

Dexter

Dexter-Chelsea Road

52

Dexter-Chelsea Road

Chelsea

94

94

Chelsea-Manchester Road

Parker Road

Scio Church Road

Chelsea Road), a two-lane highway with wide shoulders for cyclists. Turn left onto M52, and follow it to the town of Chelsea.

For a shortcut back to your ending point in Dexter, turn left past the railroad tracks behind the old Chelsea train station. In about a block, you will be able to re-cross the tracks and connect with Dexter-Chelsea Road. Dexter is about 6.5 miles away on relatively flat roads from this point.

To continue on the main route, ride through Chelsea and past I-94 to Scio Church Road. Turn left onto Scio Church Road, and follow it for 7 miles to Parker Road. Turn left onto Parker Road. In 3 miles, the road re-crosses the interstate, and, in another 3 miles, there is an A&W restaurant. Turn right at the intersection into downtown Dexter, where your trip began.

RIDE GUIDE

★   0.0 From the Dexter Clock in Dexter, ride north on Central Street.
　　0.3 The route becomes Main Street.
　　0.6 The route becomes Dexter-Pinckney Road.
　　0.9 Ride through the traffic light and onto Island Lake Road.
★   3.6 Turn right onto Dexter-Townhall Road.
★   6.5 Turn left onto North Territorial Road.
★   8.0 Turn right onto Hankerd Road.
　　10.1 The route changes names to Glenbrook.
★   11.7 At the T intersection, turn left onto Patterson Lake Road.
★   13.2 Turn left onto Doyle Road.
★   15.5 Turn left onto Unadilla Road.
★   16.7 Turn left onto Kaiser Road.
★   16.8 Turn right onto Hadley Road.
　　20.0 The route becomes Stofer Road.
★   21.4 Turn right onto Island Lake Road.
★   21.9 Turn left onto Werkner Road.
★   24.2 Turn left onto Stockbridge-Chelsea Road (M52).
　　25.5 Chelsea. The route becomes Chelsea-Manchester Road.
★   29.4 Turn left onto Scio Church Road.
★   36.0 Turn left onto Parker Road.
★   41.1 Turn right onto Dexter-Chelsea Road.
★   41.5 Turn right onto Central Street.
　　41.7 Dexter Clock. End of ride.

Hines Trail

Submitted by Charles P. Morris

This is said to rate among the most beautiful fall rides in Michigan. Hines Drive, the backbone of the Middle Rouge Parkway Bikeway system, is a parkway that runs through several Detroit suburbs, and so is considered a local treasure by the hundreds of thousands of residents who enjoy ready access to it. The greenway proper, which also includes a separated bike path (still under development), developed recreation facilities, and undeveloped woods and meadows, encompasses some 2,600 acres.

Type of ride: road bike
Starting point: the east end of the Hines Parkway, in Dearborn Heights at Ford Road
Finishing point: just south of Northville Downs racetrack in Northville
Distance: 19 miles
Level of difficulty: easy, with two significant grades
General terrain: flat to moderately hilly
Traffic conditions: moderate. On "Saturdays in the Park," between 9:00 A.M. and 3:30 P.M. throughout the summer, a 6-mile stretch

Nankin Mills Nature Center (photo by: Charles Morris)

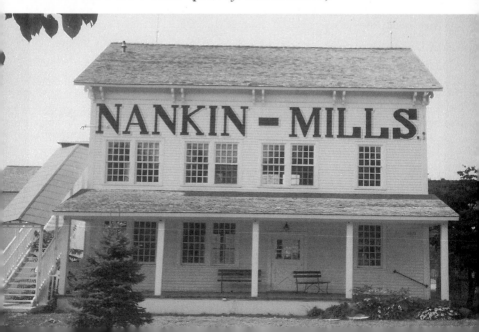

of Hines Drive between Outer Drive and Ann Arbor Trail is closed to vehicular traffic. Six at-grade crossings are encountered along the road, all of them controlled with traffic lights. Hines Drive passes under all the other roads and railroad tracks.

Estimated riding time: 2 hours

Best season/time of day to ride: September–October; Saturday and Sunday

Points of interest: This is a wonderful lakeside and riverside ride, especially beautiful in the fall, running through parts of the cities of Dearborn Heights, Westland, Livonia, Plymouth, and Northville. Attractions include the old Henry Ford village mills, initiated by Ford in order to slow the migration of country folks to the city during the Industrial Revolution. Five dams, and their resultant lakes, are encountered. These were used to power Ford's small factories and mills. River and lake views are abundant, and wildlife such as Canadian geese and raccoons are likely to be spotted. Morning breakfast rides, starting in Dearborn Heights and ending at one of several eateries in Northville, are popular among local cyclists.

Accommodations and services: all services available, including a bike shop in Northville; no camping along the parkway

Supplemental maps or other information: Middle Rouge Parkway Bikeway, available from Wayne County Parks, 33175 Ann Arbor Trail, Westland, MI 48185

GETTING THERE

In Detroit, exit the Southfield Freeway (M39) and go west 1.7 miles on Ford Road.

IN THE SADDLE

Hines Drive is the namesake of Edward D. Hines, who operated a Detroit printing business in the late 1800s and early 1900s. Few individuals in history have been better suited to have a parkway named after them: Along with Henry Ford and several others, Hines was one of the original members of the Wayne County Road Commission when it was created in 1906, at a time when there was not a single mile of improved road in the Detroit area.

Henry Ford understood that his fledgling automobile business would grow only if there were sufficient roads to drive on—hence, his

A pristine view from the Hines Trail (photo by: Charles Morris)

interest in building a system of roads. Hines, in the meantime, was an early cycling enthusiast who served as president of the League of American Wheelmen during its turn-of-the-century heyday, and he was a pioneer leader of the League's "good roads movement." During Hines's thirty-three-year stint on the road commission, some fourteen million yards of concrete were poured, creating 2,500 miles of roads in Wayne County. The county's model road system would be emulated by many other areas of the country.

One other legacy of Edward Hines can be seen on the vast majority of the world's paved roads. It is said that one day, as he watched a horse-drawn milk wagon meandering down a country lane, with milk splashing overboard and onto the road, Hines conceived the idea of striping roads with white paint for traffic-control purposes. He tested his road striping scheme in the Detroit area, and from there the concept spread far and wide.

The parkway follows the Middle Rouge River, crossing it at several points. Wide, blacktopped shoulders run on either side of the two-lane road; there is also a paved bike path that runs much of the length of the park.

To get started, ride northwest onto Hines Drive from its intersection with Ford Road. Eleven recreational facilities—with picnic tables, slides, ball diamonds, restrooms, and drinking water—will be found along the way. These facilities are Parkland at mile 0.7, Helm's Haven at mile 1.5, Parr at mile 2.6, Perrin Field at mile 5.1, Merriman Hollow at mile 7.5, Hawthorne at mile 8, Nankin Mills at mile 8.6, Levan Knoll at mile 10.6, Newburgh Point at mile 12.4, Wilcox Pond at mile 15.5, and Northville at mile 18.6.

Nankin Mills, at 8.6 miles, is the first old mill encountered. Once a grist mill and later a Ford factory, it now serves as park headquarters and a nature center. The original mill was built on the site between 1835 and 1842, with a replacement built soon after the Civil War. In 1918, Henry Ford purchased the mill as part of his plan to develop village industries along the Rouge and other nearby rivers. Using a turbine generator, Nankin Mills produced carburetors and other parts for Ford's early cars.

A canoe livery on Nankin Pond at 9 miles provides floating access to approximately 3 miles of the river, as far as the dam at Newburgh. At mile 13.1, just before you pass under I-275, a blacktopped bike path heads south, providing a side trip to the Monroe County line. Cross Northville Road at 16.4 miles; a 0.5-mile side trip south on this road will take you into the old town of Plymouth, an area brimming with quaint stores and craft shops. Just past the M14 bridge, you will see another blacktopped bike path going east along M14. This curves north to follow I-275 to 10 Mile and Grand River.

At mile 17.1, pass an old stone structure remaining from Mead's Mill. The parkway ends at 7 Mile Road; 0.1 mile to the right from this point you will find a well-deserved ice cream stand. To the left 0.5 mile, just past the Northville Downs, is Northville, another interesting old town worth visiting. There is a bike shop here, along with several good restaurants.

RIDE GUIDE
★ 0.0 From the east end of the trail at the border of Dearborn and Dearborn Heights on Ford Road, ride west on Hines Drive.
  9.0 Nankin Pond.
  12.4 Newburgh Point.
  15.5 Wilcox Road.
  16.4 Cross Northville Road.
  17.1 Mead's Mill historic marker.
  19.0 7 Mile Road. End of ride.

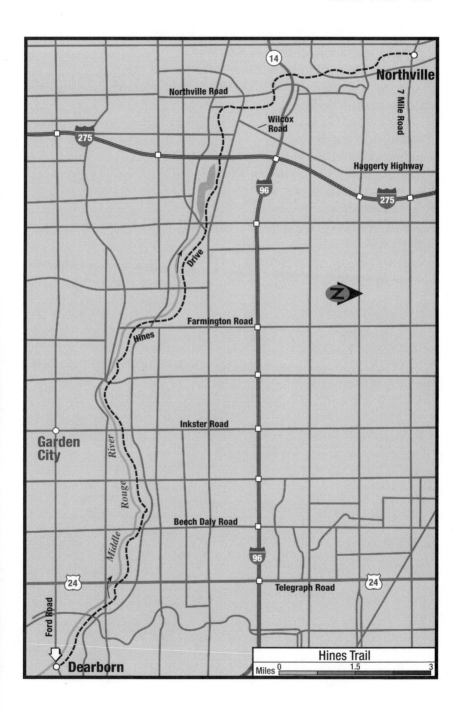

Père Marquette Trail
Submitted by Edward Elliott

Travel on a former railroad right-of-way from Midland through the countryside to Coleman.

Type of ride: road bike
Starting point: southwest side of Midland
Finishing point: Coleman
Distance: 20.3 miles, one way
Level of difficulty: moderate
General terrain: paved rail-trail from Midland to Coleman
Traffic conditions: light

Herbert H. Dow Historical Museum (photo by: Edward Elliott)

Estimated riding time: 2 hours
Best season/time of day to ride: April through October
Points of interest: There are museums in Midland, Sanford, and
    Coleman. Many of the trail features, including paving, signs, and
    benches, are made from recycled materials collected locally.
Accommodations and services: food and bike services available along
    the route
Supplemental maps or other information: none

GETTING THERE

The starting point is on the three-sided bridge on the railroad right-of-
way at the southwest end of Ashman Street in Midland. To reach Midland from Saginaw, drive 55 miles north on I-75; turn left (west) onto
US 10 at exit 162. Go 12 miles west on US 10.

IN THE SADDLE

Begin the route at the Tridge, a three-sided bridge at the juncture of
the Tittibawassee and Chippewa Rivers, and follow the trail to the northwest. At this point, the trail is paved. It passes under the Mark Putnam
Bridge along Main Street and into Emerson Park. This area is flooded
at least once a year, but damage is limited due to the location and construction of the park. Past the park, cross the Sturgeon Creek Bridge,
an original rail structure reworked to allow bike and trail traffic.

The next section of the trail passes the Overlook rest stop, located
along a natural wetland area. At about 3 miles are a bike shop and other
services. At 5.8 miles is the Averhill Rollaway at an overlook of the
Tittibawassee River. This area was once used to stockpile logs for the
spring drive down the river to sawmills at Midland and Saginaw.

At 8.3 miles is the village of Sanford, which includes services for
trail users one block off the trail along Main Street. Moving west from
Sanford, you will cross the Tittibawassee River, and then the Big Salt
River on two of the original railroad bridges. At the 10.5-mile point
is the Arbutus Bog boardwalk. This boardwalk extends from the trail
bypass out into a typical northern temperate zone bog. Pitcher plants,
leatherleaf, cranberry bushes, and more can all be seen here.

As you travel farther to the west, the character of the trail changes,
and the land becomes more agricultural. Farm fields are now the
dominant feature. You will cross the Big Salt River once more; then

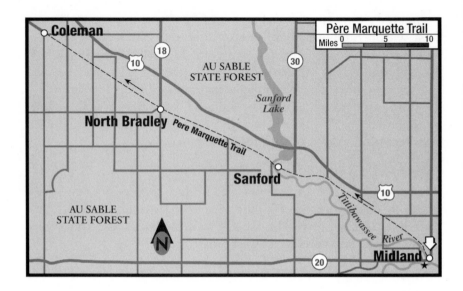

proceed to North Bradley at the 15-mile point. (There are currently no facilities available in North Bradley.)

Proceeding for 7 more miles, you will arrive in Coleman at the 22-mile point. The grain elevators in Coleman are evidence of the agricultural importance of this part of the state. There is a restaurant located just north of the trail as it intersects the main road in Coleman. Have a bite before your pickup car arrives, or retrace your route for a 44-mile loop.

RIDE GUIDE

★   0.0 From the Tridge in Midland, ride west on the Père
        Marquette Rail-Trail.
    2.9 The Bradley House.
    5.8 Dublin Road.
    8.3 Averhill Rollaway.
    10.5 Sanford.
    14.8 North Bradley.
    22.0 Coleman. End of ride.

Index

About the Contributors

Bruce and Fran Baker have ridden their Santana tandem in twenty-five U.S. states, plus Canada and the Netherlands. Their favorite places to ride are the last place they went and the next place they are going. Bruce submitted both Ride 17 (Cadillac Slide) and Ride 20 (Manistee Forest Ride). Fran and Bruce have been members of Adventure Cycling for eight years.

Judith Briggs has been an active cyclist for several years and a member of Adventure Cycling for three years. Judith submitted Ride 16 (Mission Loop).

Vern Cascaddan has ridden his route, Ride 26 (Lake Michigan Trek), on an organized trip and recommends it to everyone who enjoys bicycle touring. Vern has been a member of Adventure Cycling for one year.

Dan Dalquist is an avid cyclist who rides as often as his bank president position permits. He has been a member of Adventure Cycling for one year. Dan submitted both Ride 3 (Keweenaw Trek) and Ride 5 (Calumet Loop).

Russ and Jane Dykstra can often be seen riding their handmade tandem recumbent trike through the streets of Holland, Michigan. Russ is also a full-time commuter on his handmade hybrid bike. They have been members of Adventure Cycling for six years. Jane and Russ submitted Ride 30 (Holland-Saugatuck Connection).

Edward Elliott served as chairperson of the advisory board that planned and built the Père Marquette Trail, featured in Ride 39. He has been cycling for thirty years and commutes to work daily on two wheels during the summer. Edward has been a member of Adventure Cycling for one year.

Alan Fark is a family physician yearning for extra time to get out and ride the trails. The highlights of his cycling career are two tours through Japan. Alan submitted both Ride 1 (Grand Island Shuffle) and Ride 14 (Shingle Mill Pathway). He has been a member of Adventure Cycling for six years.

Karl Fava, who has been riding for several years now, submitted Ride 9 (North Lake Trek). Karl has been a member of Adventure Cycling for four years.

Kerry Irons has been cycle touring since the late 1960s. From long-distance, self-contained tours to light-bike/heavy-wallet tours with his wife Mary, he has ridden in twenty-eight states and seven different countries. Kerry submitted Ride 21 (Harbor Springs Loop). He has been a member of Adventure Cycling for eighteen years.

Laurie James, who submitted Ride 25 (Ludington Trek), has been riding for ten years. She enjoys doing one or two tours per summer, along with a few century rides. Laurie has been a member of Adventure Cycling for two years.

Lew Kidder, who submitted Ride 32 (Ann Arbor Century), has been an Adventure Cycling member for sixteen years. He has been active in the triathlon movement, having founded *Triathlon Today* (now *Inside Triathlon*), one of the sport's two national publications.

Terry Kureth has been a member of Adventure Cycling for seven years. Both he and his wife Ann agree that Ride 19 (Harbor Springs Tour) is one of their favorites.

Alexander McGarry, an Adventure Cycling member for one year, submitted Ride 33 (Paint Creek Trail). He enjoys riding and running with his three adult daughters. In addition to cross-state bike rides, Alex also enjoys competing in marathons.

Michael J. McPhillips and his family submitted Ride 11 (Cadillac Pathway). Mike, Laurie, Michael, Christopher, and Nickolas have been enjoying mountain biking for three years and have taken single-day, family rides all over the state of Michigan.

Charles Morris is a seventy-one-year-old retiree who travels at least part of the ride he submitted—Ride 38 (Hines Trail)—every day. He has been a member of Adventure Cycling for four years.

Joy and Aribert Neumann, members of Adventure Cycling for one year, submitted both Ride 35 (Bald Mountain Trail) and Ride 36 (Lake Orion Trail). They have completed a self-contained, cross-country bike tour, as well as several shorter tours.

Carol Otto has been riding mountain and road bikes for five years but definitely prefers her mountain bike. Carol submitted both Ride 22 (Green Lake Loop) and Ride 31 (Pinckney Dirt Ride). She has been a member of Adventure Cycling for two years.

Don Parry, a road cyclist for ten years now, is a new member of Adventure Cycling. He submitted Ride 18 (Bellaire Century), a ride that he has completed every year since 1988.

John Prius has been regularly cycling for twenty-four years, including self-contained tours and a number of centuries. He has been a member of Adventure Cycling for four years. John submitted Ride 24 (Last Train to Clarksville).

Thomas Rea, a member of Adventure Cycling for two years, submitted Ride 12 (Torch Lake Loop). Thomas rates this ride in the rolling countryside as one of his favorite places to pedal.

Ken and Viki Shayna have been cycling together since Viki had a crazy idea to bike in Europe in 1983; this subsequently led to a tour of the United States in 1988. They now do cross-country trips in their dreams and pedal around Michigan with their two sons, Adam and Devin. Ken and Viki, members of Adventure Cycling for ten years, submitted Ride 37 (Dexter Ramble).

Greg and Bobbie Simon are experienced tandem cyclists, although they do occasionally like to get out and explore Michigan's cross-country ski trails on their mountain bikes. They submitted Ride 15 (Lake Leelanau Loop). Greg and Bobbie have been members of

Adventure Cycling for one year.

Teri Simpson, a flight nurse and graduate student, has been riding for the past five years. She enjoys training for and competing in the National 24-Hour Challenge. Terri submitted Ride 29 (Paw Paw Way). She has been a member of Adventure Cycling for five years.

Arthur Souter, who has been cycling for several years now, submitted Ride 28 (Coopersville Ramble), one of his favorite rides. He has been an Adventure Cycling member for ten years.

Michael Sproul, who submitted Ride 27 (Kal-Haven Trail), has been a member of Adventure Cycling for two years. Michael has been actively cycling for the past ten years and enjoys riding with his children, nieces, and nephews.

John Stevens, a professor at a local university, enjoys touring in the eastern part of the Upper Peninsula with his daughter, Meg. He has been a member of Adventure Cycling for five years. He submitted Ride 4 (Mackinac Island Tour), Ride 7 (Cedarville Shuffle), and Ride 10 (St. Ignace Trek).

Michael Vanderveen submitted Ride 23 (Grand Haven Trail). He has been a member of Adventure Cycling for two years. Michael is a weekend rider around the West Michigan area who dreams of doing a long cross-country trip.

Robert Weishaupt has been actively cycling since 1978. He has ridden in forty-two states and is a director and past chairperson of the League of Michigan Bicyclists. Robert, who has been a member of Adventure Cycling for seven years, submitted Ride 34 (Tip of the Thumb Run).

Gary Wisely has been a member of Adventure Cycling for one year and enjoys annual, week-long, self-supported bike tours of the Upper Peninsula. All this is leading up to a longer tour when he retires. Gary submitted four rides: Ride 2 (Newberry Ramble), Ride 6 (Mass City Loop), Ride 8 (Escanaba Explorer), and Ride 13 (Mio Ride).

THE MOUNTAINEERS, founded in 1906, is a nonprofit outdoor activity and conservation club, whose mission is "to explore, study, preserve, and enjoy the natural beauty of the outdoors. . . . " Based in Seattle, Washington, the club is now the third-largest such organization in the United States, with 15,000 members and five branches throughout Washington State.

The Mountaineers sponsors both classes and year-round outdoor activities in the Pacific Northwest, which include hiking, mountain climbing, ski-touring, snowshoeing, bicycling, camping, kayaking and canoeing, nature study, sailing, and adventure travel. The club's conservation division supports environmental causes through educational activities, sponsoring legislation, and presenting informational programs. All club activities are led by skilled, experienced volunteers, who are dedicated to promoting safe and responsible enjoyment and preservation of the outdoors.

If you would like to participate in these organized outdoor activities or the club's programs, consider a membership in The Mountaineers. For information and an application, write or call The Mountaineers, Club Headquarters, 300 Third Avenue West, Seattle, Washington 98119; (206) 284-6310.

The Mountaineers Books, an active, nonprofit publishing program of the club, produces guidebooks, instructional texts, historical works, natural history guides, and works on environmental conservation. All books produced by The Mountaineers are aimed at fulfilling the club's mission.

Send or call for our catalog of more than 300 outdoor titles:

 The Mountaineers Books
1001 SW Klickitat Way, Suite 201
Seattle, WA 98134
1-800-553-4453 / e-mail: mbooks@mountaineers.org